Abhay Singh

Body, Mind & Spirit

Publish & Print
www.publishandprint.co.uk

I THANK YOU

Who are you?

Where are you?

What are you?

I know, you are there.

Always... always.

Always with me.

Protecting me...

And my loved ones.

As always.

I THANK YOU!!!

My Dear wife Anju...

You are my Angel.

Following me.

With love.

With compassion.

You are more than I asked for.

I THANK YOU!!!

If you Anju, are my Angel. You, Rashmi, Neha, Radha and Rahul and of course my lovely little grandchildren Aanya, Dylan, Joshua and Alex are the bright lights from the angelic world shining on me showing right direction. Darpan, Darragh and Chris holding on to the pillars against the devils of the kalyuga.

I THANK YOU!!!

While rest of my family and my friends... you all, I know, were in my thoughts praying always for my wellbeing.

I THANK YOU!!!

I am very grateful for your contributions in various ways and made this book a reality.

I THANK YOU!!!

And finally, the entire team of N H S ROYAL GLAMORGAN HOSPITAL WALES.

For your dedication commitment and care 24 hours a day.

In saving my life.

I THANK YOU!!!

"The book Mind Body & Spirit authored by a very close and dear friend of mine of nearly 50 years is a snapshot of his journey beginning with his travel from his home town in India to UK, his marriage to a typical young Indian village girl, his sojourn in Nigeria and birth of his three beautiful daughters there, and finally returning back and settling in the UK.

A good portion of the book deals in detail the trials and tribulations, ups and downs, and the life threatening and near-death experiences. The chapter Roller-Coaster Ride by his daughter Neha beautifully captures hospital events, suffering and fear, and the joy and relief of her dad making it through. How important is the family support in healing and recovery of a family member is very well described and emphasized.

The author has attempted to, based on his belief and understanding of the Hindu mythology, address the metaphysical question of the nature of mind. Reading through the pages it becomes distinctly clear how the body, mind & spirit are interlinked and interwoven; how one affects the other. A deep influence of Hindu traditions, rituals, and Gods is manifest in the writings. An element of quantum physics, supported by statements of eminent physicists and renowned writers, has been used to further elaborate the interrelationship of mind, body & spirit and with the entire cosmos.

Although the book is a personal account it serves to illustrate how fallible and fragile a human being is or can be, but at the same time the same person can use his will power, faith, and determination to turn things around... that is the power of mind over body.

Having had the privilege of knowing the author very closely, I can relate to many aspects and facets narrated in this book. I have personally liked reading the book, and congratulate the author for a marvelous effort to put down in print his life experiences and understanding of nature and cosmos.

I rate this book 8 out of 10."

Prem Prakash Rai
Auckland, New Zealand
8 February 2021

Contents

BODY, MIND AND SPIRIT

SYNOPSIS

The society in which we live somehow dictates what we do in our lives. I am 71 years old and this is my first attempt to write a book. My interest in writing has been hidden in me since my childhood. As a young boy I was short and timid, keeping away from those hard and tough and the blessed ones trying to win the race.

- *Where are you?*
- *What are you?*
- *Who are you?*
- *I know you are there*
- *Always with me.*
- *Protecting me. Guiding me.*

The quest for the answers to these burning questions led me, today, to write this book. I must confess that the writing of this book involves deep understanding of various disciplines of science, theology, humanity and of course the wisdom of ancient India.

My understanding of all these disciplines are very basic and therefore I had to rely on the expertise of others to

1

make my own understanding and imagination. It makes it easy to ask for forgiveness because we all know that my understanding and imagination is subject to my own preconditioned subconscious mind.

The ancient Indian saints and sages described the universe to be, made of five different elements; Kshiti, Jal, Pawak, Gagan and Sameer. They are the Sanskrit words meaning in English soil, water, fire, sky and air.

Lord Krishna, some 5000 years ago, described himself as God and said, 'He is the creator of the universe and He is also the part of creation. He is everywhere in the creation. He is indestructible.'

Water cannot wet Him, air cannot blow Him, fire cannot burn Him, or weapons cannot cut Him.

The scientists today, describe universe as matter and energy. 70% of the universe is dark energy, 25% is dark matter. Dark matter and dark energy do not respond to the world as we see and therefore cannot be measured.

Out of the remaining 5% less than 1% is the matter as we experience it: the trees, the mountains, the rivers, the sun, the moon and any object we perceive with our five senses; the sense of touch, taste, smell, sound and seeing.

The observable universe may also be divided into organic and inorganic matter. Organic matter evolved slowly into living organisms from amoeba to plants and animals of great diversity. All living organisms are made of small units called cells. These small units are made of basic subatomic particles the electrons, the protons and the neutrons. So are the inorganic substances. These particles are of +ve, -ve and neutral charge. So, the whole universe is a system of electrons protons and neutrons intricately balanced with each other and with the rest of the cosmos. Another interesting feature of these elementary particles is, that they behave both like solid particles as well as wave like energy. This has been demonstrated several times over the years by many physicists by an experiment famously known as "double slit experiment".

The observable solid world, therefore is only an interpretational experience by our minds and does not really exist. However, common in all these is Energy.

Everything is Energy. Nothing other than energy. Energy which cannot be destroyed but can only be transformed from one form to another. I am, therefore, energy like you, like that, like the tree, like the river, like the mountain.

Once I exist... I exist. I do not really die. I change form and come back again and again age after age. According to my Karmic account.

INTRODUCTION

Maybe I am being childish in thinking that I too can write a book one day, which someone will read and appreciate. My interest in writing goes back to my school days. By now, I am used to getting negative or half-hearted sympathetic feedback or perhaps, they were all trying to help me in their own way. I remember, once my father making a remark...

"FATAA HAAL HOGA. FATICHER RAHEGA.
ZINDAGI BHAR TOO HINDI KA TEACHER RAHEGA."

(Meaning, if you carry on like this you will become a teacher of HINDI but have no money).

My attachment for literature never completely went. A friend of my father-in-law was a palm reader. One day he read my palm, sitting casually with us, having tea and snacks and predicted that I am going to write a book one day.

Write a book? I, kind of, closed the topic and moved on with the conversation.

During the latter part of my educational career, I developed an interest in body, mind and spirit. But I never really thought that this would take me anywhere. I couldn't even dare. Yet here I am now, giving it a go. Trying to make the two dreams come true.

The year 1971 was a turning point in my life. I can't forget that train journey from Pirpainti to Delhi via Bhagalpur and then the flight from New Delhi to Heathrow London.

I was flying high in the sky. Looking down through the window trying to find a grip underneath like a kite lost in the sky.

It wasn't easy then. It had never been, I must say. And then I got married to a young, charming village girl from India in 1974. All I can say is that there is a saying, "Marriages are destined in heaven and performed on Earth."

I was in India for over two months during the marriage and it went like it was meant to be. To me I was marrying someone who was the daughter of a reputable farmer of high recognition in the society. The big house surrounding a large farmland with a jeep and a tractor and of course, the usual farmers crowd. Looked very impressive. It was a family consisting of my wife, her two elder sisters with their husbands, her father, mother grandmother and a three years old boy from her elder sister. And the cows, the buffaloes, the mango trees, the guava trees and I must not forget the Cheera Meera flower which she had a special interest in showing me whenever she got a chance to escape from the eyes of the crowd. I personally felt myself out of place in all this. I felt better in the presence of my father-in-law, in the same way that I used to feel safer with my teacher in the classroom during my school days. He is no more with us and I can understand now, why I felt like that.

As we two were beginning to enjoy each other's attention the time to come back to the UK was approaching, and the development of a relationship was becoming more and more evident. She had a habit of walking bare-footed. I used to take pride in asking her not to walk without slippers or buying cough syrup for her when she got a cold or paracetamol when she had a headache. She was beginning to feel more than what I could understand.

The remaining few days of my stay was in Delhi, where

one day I had to visit someone on my own. I was late coming back to the hotel. As I entered my room, I saw her sitting alone waiting for me without having her afternoon lunch while others went to the cinema. I was touched. We spent the afternoon together with not many exchanges of words but many tears. She says, she fell in love with me that afternoon while I was still struggling to find a meaning to my feelings and emotions. With a promise to write to her and a promise for a reply from her, I left that night for the UK.

She, finally came to join me here in the UK in 1975 a year after. I remember at Heathrow airport, the immigration officer announcing my name. As I climbed up the escalator and approached the officer, I saw her sitting with some other ladies. I waved to her. She waved back at me. As she came closer to me, I was absorbing the situation by recalling my marital obligations and responsibilities ahead. At the same time, I could read into her eyes the pain and sufferings of leaving her loved ones back home and courage to say, "Here I am all yours." Who is she? Where did she come from? I can't help wondering sometimes.

As a young boy I was timid, short and weighed only 10

stone. Though relatively good in my studies, I rather preferred to sit on the back-bench of the class room and felt safer when the teacher was around. That someone is protecting me while in school or at home or in the village or walking the streets or travelling by bicycle, bus or train. Sometimes like a friend or a relative or someone I had never met before, or sometimes as an unforeseen, unexplained source. Perhaps that source gave me some strength for what I would do in my life.

I decided to go to Nigeria for teaching, where we had three beautiful children, travelling various parts of Nigeria and Europe there on facing difficult situations sometimes potentially life threatening for over 9 years. Yes, someone has always been there with me, protecting me.

Talking about traveling, when I reached the age of 16, it was the age of traveling for finding places in the institutes for higher learning. Something that everyone had to learn. You must be fit and sporty. I still only weighed 10 stone and my trouser size was 28 inches × 28 inches... I did play football and badminton in school days though.

I think I had enough qualifications for the job. Soon enough it was time for action. I had to change trains from one railway platform to another, rushed with my suitcase in my right hand containing all the essentials for overnight stay and necessary documents. I was holding the suitcase tight. At the same time, my eyes were everywhere especially for the man behind me. I had all the reasons to believe that he was after my suitcase.

With my left hand I was checking my top pocket for my ticket and back pocket for my wallet too. I could see the train moving as I changed my gear of speed. Well done, I gave myself a pat on my back as I got hold of the train's gate bar with my left hand and managed to squeeze one foot on the step of the train. O my God! That man was right behind me. As I fastened my grip on the suitcase, the train started picking up speed. I was sweating. The train was packed full. No place to move forward or backward. I soon started feeling the strain of the suitcase, which was getting heavier by the minute. It was my first new leather suitcase. My mum warned me, "Do not lose it," as she fed me farewell yogurt and sugar for a safe journey. I was getting desperate for help. The man behind me, very cleverly, was trying to be sympathetic. He asked me to concentrate on moving forward while he took care of the suitcase. With the corner of my eyes I tried to capture a quick description of the man. He was tall, dark and wearing a white shirt, well built, weighed certainly much more than 10 stone. I was left with no choice but to follow instructions. I moved forward and to my surprise he pushed my suitcase from behind. It worked. I managed to get in and drag my suitcase in behind me. It was a great relief. Then I offered my 10 stone hand (I mean in proportion) to lift him inside. He declined saying that he was getting down at the next station. He will manage. Soon the next station came. Old passengers got down. I found a place to sit and a safe place for my suitcase too. As I relaxed to the usual music and noise of a typical Indian railway station from chai wala selling tea to paanwala snack stalls. Newspaper and roasted monkey nuts... to paani pande, the drinking water man with bucket full of water supplying water to drink, going compartment to compartment, from one end to other end of the station. Soon the train left for its next destination, fully packed. As the train picked up speed and the usual music and noise of the station was swept away by the noise of the speedy train on its next mission, leaving behind an empty station for the next train. Trains come and go. Each train is unique. Each train contains its own stories leaving behind an empty station with the stationmaster who is always there monitoring every train until his duty ceases to be.

I can't help thinking about that man... dark, tall, wearing a white shirt, well-built and weighing certainly more than 10 stone.

In 1978 we were blessed with our first daughter. We took her to Bhagalpur, India on a family visit. She was only a few months old and was very pretty. One day, as we were going out with my sisters and brothers for an evening out, the rickshaw was fast, perhaps the driver was drunk. It collided with another rickshaw. We were thrown away all over the road. Fortunately, the truck stopped just on time. Only my sister can say how close my precious little daughter was from the tyre of the truck when she picked her up. I was upset. I was angry. I sent everyone home. Asked them to send some help while I was holding the rickshaw driver. Crowds were gathering without having any intimidating effect on me. I don't know where the strength came from. Because I was still only weighing 10 stone and wore 28 inches x 28 inches trousers.

In 1986 we finally decided to leave Nigeria to settle in the UK. By this time, we had two more beautiful daughters. Settling in the UK was a struggle but fine.

Between myself and my wife we managed to keep a roof over our heads and food on the table. Time passed by and soon it was time for my eldest daughter to get married. During the marriage ceremony I was giving a speech. And in that speech, I mentioned about taking all our three daughters to a swimming pool. The special feature of the swimming pool was that it had a wave like functions which they used to create in order to amuse the swimmers. It was frightening for the first-time visitors as the sound of siren filled the emptiness, all the three children came to me frightened and crying and held me tight. They had faith in me. I will not let her drown no matter what! I, with one hand, was holding all the three while with other hand I was holding the side bar of the pool. Tides came and went. Nothing happened. I was the hero. Later, during the speech I apologized with them and said, "My children, I was equally worried, as I can't swim myself ." Can't swim? They all laughed. I explained why? My father was a police officer, officer-in-charge of a police station. It was a frequently transferable job. Wherever he went, we had to follow. That's one of the reasons I didn't have an established friendship with anyone.

One of the police stations where we lived there was a river flowing nearby. On a hot afternoon I decided to go for a dip. There were few people around too. As I had my first dip, someone asked; "Can't you swim?" No, I replied. He offered to help me learn. I accepted. He held me from one hand and dragged me to the deep water. He put his one hand under my chest and asked me to stroke my hands and legs in the water. It didn't work. Went out of control. He soon left me going up and down on my own gasping for breath. My lungs were getting filled with water as I struggled for oxygen. I could see my death only moments away. But I didn't die. Someone from the other side of the river jumped in and rescued me. I only vaguely remember his face now. But he saved my life. Since then I never tried to learn swimming.

I have experienced many situations like this in my life for which I will be very happy to find a meaningful explanation. The most recent being my last major illness involving reoccurring pneumonia complicated further by heart failure. A period which changed my life.

This is best explained in my daughter's note to me as follows..."

ROLLERCOASTER RIDE

To our dearest papa!

Our journey with you on this rollercoaster ride began on the 30th January 2018 when you were admitted to hospital ward 6 as a result of another pneumonia infection. On Friday 9th February that last text message we got from you saying the doctors were sending you home next week as the pneumonia was clearing...

Saturday 17th February 2018

It is now 1 week since you were transferred to the ITU (intensive treatment unit) by Dr Don Hunford, who saw you in ward 6 that day and with little observation on your breathing difficulties immediately referred you to ITU ward around 2pm on Saturday 10th February. They put you on the Opti flow warm O2 machine and within a couple of hours mum could see an improvement. You were on the best ward in the hospital with so many nice nurses monitoring your breathing and bloods the minute you arrived. That night for the first time in a week and a half you felt a lot more relaxed and safer. Before that you were in isolation ward 6 with no sign of any nurses at times except for your guardian Angel, your wife... our dearest mummy who would not leave your side not even at night. That night you told mummy to go home as you were much happier with the 5 star treatment by the ITU nurses.

In the early hours (2 to 3am) of Sunday the 11th February we all got the 'dreaded phone call', one by one we were told that you suffered two cardiac arrests each one three minutes long and the ITU team were successful in reviving you both times, the ECG showed no damage to the heart and everything was functioning fine. They also told us that the next 24 to 48 hours was critical and that it was not looking good.

As you can imagine we were all extremely distressed with the thought of losing you and especially our dearest mummy who couldn't even move or speak with the shock. One could see and hear the pain and fear in her eyes and her voice.

That morning I booked the earliest flight from Dublin and arrived (without my sons Alex and Dylan) at the hospital by 1pm and was by your side with mummy and Rahul (my brother). All the way I was praying and praying that nothing bad would happen. The others...

mum, Radha, Lilly (my two sisters) and Rahul were already there since early hours of the morning praying also that what the consultants were telling them was not true and trying to make sense of all this and why this had happened to you.

Every minute was crucial in your road to recovery and eventually those minutes turned into 48 hours, at this point your infection, blood gases and breathing (without ventilator) had improved significantly since Saturday and even the nurses were giving us positive signals...

On Tuesday the 13th February (Pancake Day), when Darragh my husband, was baking pancakes for Alex and Dylan in Dublin, we were anxiously waiting for some good news here in Royal Glamorgan Hospital as they decided to wake you up.

Slowly but surely, we could see you trying to move and wake up. Every two seconds the nurses and each one of us, while visiting, were reassuring you of where you were and preparing you for the removal of that awkward tube from your mouth and throat leading to your lungs. Around 4pm that day Chris 'the nurse' woke you up with his very loud voice. Me, Radha and mummy watched you open your eyes slowly... it was such a struggle as you did seem like you were really enjoying your sleep, something you have not done in the past year.

Eventually you did manage to keep them open with our reassuring words and familiar voices confirming that you were well and how proud we were of you for fighting this. Mummy kept praying 'Om Shanti'. You could also hear her chanting. Unfortunately, we had to leave you at that point as the doctors and nurses were going to pull the tube out of your mouth as they thought you were ready to breathe again by yourself without much ventilator support.

All your blood results were good, and level of infection seemed contained.

For that hour, your children and wife waited anxiously in the waiting room next door. We held our hands together and prayed to God that we would see you awake and talking soon... that hour felt like a lifetime. Then we saw two doctors and Chris the nurse come in through the door. Dr Ceri Lynch explained that when the tube came out you were responding very well and seemed quite relaxed however they could see that your heart rate was dropping and eventually it came to a stop.

They immediately performed CPR and revived you back to life again... this time your heart stopped for about two minutes! They had to put the tube back in through your mouth for ventilation and sedated you to make you more comfortable. We were shocked with this news and so disappointed that we could not see you awake but they reassured us that they could fix the problem by inserting a pacemaker under your skin where the wires from the box would be connected to your heart and would send signals to keep pumping if your own natural hearts pacemaker was to stop again. This fix came with risks, they explained, as this required general anaesthesia as well as the risk of infection was always there.

We knew this was the only option for you. In further consultation with the cardiologist, Jon, he assured us that this would be a straightforward surgery and was quite confident that the risks were minimal with a significant benefit to your precious life and we agreed... never did we want to hear the words 'cardiac arrest' again!

On Friday 16th February, around 11am you were carefully sent down to surgery while connected to the ventilator for the pacemaker procedure. I was back in Dublin at this stage with my two boys and Radha and her husband Chris were in the hospital making sure all went to plan. Mummy, Lilly and Rahul all waited anxiously once again to hear the news. Shortly after 1pm Radha texted to let us know that everything went to plan, you were doing fine and back in ITU recovering.

We were all so relieved and still anxious as we knew that you still weren't out of the woods and had a long way to go yet. Later that day they decided that they would try and wake you on Saturday 17th February as you needed some time to recover from surgery and another day to fight the infection. Your temperature was slightly raised and so was your inflammatory (CPR level) marker. That day I decided to book flights to come back to Cardiff on the Saturday morning, as I was desperate to see you awake and recovering. Again I left the boys with Darragh that morning and me and Radha were by your side by 11am.

We were surprised to see you awake as the nurse told us that morning that it was unlikely they would wake you today because you were still fighting your infection and your chest X-ray wasn't great in comparison to yesterday. However, the doctors came round and decided to wake you around 10.15am regardless (the time my plane happened to land at Cardiff airport as we were half an hour delayed!). It was a miracle to see you awake and responding to our questions. You were so distressed and uncomfortable with that dreaded tube down your throat but we all kept reassuring you that it was only for short while until they pulled it out but for this to happen you needed to prove to them your breathing was fine with very little ventilator support and you were well enough to cough it out when instructed to do so.

They sent us all out to the waiting room as they were going to assess if you could cope with the excavation process. Again, we all waited anxiously in the room next door, staring at the glass in the door, Radha peeking through the window checking if the curtains were still drawn. While we waited around 2.30pm that afternoon we all heard this loud noise and felt the walls and windows shaking like someone slammed all the doors shut with such force. 'A tremor,' Chris shouted and everyone immediately stood up worried for minute it was an earthquake or something. No one else was panicking or running out so we all just sat back down, I checked the news five minutes later and they confirmed it was an earthquake of 4.4 magnitude, epicentre north of Swansea. Eventually Dr Gibson and Chris the nurse came in and told us how you were.

You were still with us however the process failed because this time your O_2/CO_2 levels depleted and you were struggling with infection, which was exhausting you. They decided to put you back to sleep and said you were happy for them to do so! For some reason the way the news was delivered to us we understood that they tried to take the tube out and although your O_2 levels started to deplete at that stage your heart rate was absolutely fine.

We were so confused with this and couldn't work out what was causing this. It was only that evening when I got chatting to a very nice lady, Liz the nurse from Aberdare, who explained exactly what happened that afternoon. Then the penny dropped, this made so much more sense and we were so pleased that there wasn't another problem or issue with your lungs causing your blood gases to deplete and it was simply that you weren't ready because you were still fighting an infection.

On Sunday 18th February they de-sedated you very early in the morning and you woke up for about thirty minutes later. Again you seemed agitated and your blood gases started to struggle after half hour so they sedated you again.

Dr Ceri Lynch explained to us that they wanted to perform a bronchoscopy. Insert a camera down the tube through your throat and into your lungs to see if they could see anything abnormal or large pockets of mucus/secretions. They also said they would flush the lungs with saline to see if that could help clear up any blockages in the air sacs of your lungs. They took a couple of samples from both lungs; one was bloody but said it was nothing to be concerned about and sent them to the microbiology lab for testing.

On Monday 19th February Dr Gibson explained that they had decided that at this stage the best option for you was a tracheostomy; another minor surgery that would be performed under general anaesthesia whereby a tube would be inserted through your throat and down your trachea. This would be connected to the ventilator instead of the tube through your mouth and would allow you to breath with assistance if needed, it would be more comfortable for you when awake and without much hesitation we all agreed to go ahead with the surgery. That afternoon you were taken down to theatre around 3.30pm and we were informed just after 4pm that all went to plan and you were on your way back to the ITU. We were so relieved once again, that evening they decided not to wake you up as they wanted to give your body rest from surgery and would gradually let the anaesthetic wear off and start reducing your sedation level to a point where you were comfortable at night.

On the morning of Tuesday 20th February (the day I was due to fly back to Dublin to see my boys,) they woke you up. They stopped the sedation early that morning and by the time I came in around 11am you were starting to come round. You were extremely groggy and were finding it very difficult to open your eyes to speak to us. You could hear us and were nodding to our questions and voices and we could see tears of pain / joy / mixed emotions from your eyes. We were so happy and relieved that once again you could understand / remember us all and there was no visible signs of damage as a result of the trauma you experienced the past week. I stayed in the hospital with you that day until 2pm and had to leave to catch my flight at 3.40pm. There was no chance of missing it with Chris's helicopter on standby to take me to airport once again. I was much happier leaving you this time as I knew you were waking, you didn't seem distressed and the nurses Vicky and Chris kept reassuring us you were doing so well with your breathing.

You were on very little ventilation support and all your blood gases and infection / inflammatory markers were normal.

As soon as I got home that evening and saw my boys again I was so happy and could see things from a bigger perspective. How lucky we were to still have you with us today living and breathing, something we were not expecting just over a week ago, the good care you were getting from the nurses and consultants (Fitzgerald, Gibson, Lynch even though some were really negative about you and your recovery) and the support from your wife and children would help you get through this.

I knew deep down you would recover from this despite the statistics and now was not your time to go. Every day you kept fighting and more importantly were getting stronger and stronger.

The coming days (20th - 22nd March) after you woke up were extremely challenging. Mentally and physically as you will hear from Mum, Rashmi, Radha, Rahul and Chris, you could not speak from the trachi tube, nor see because your glasses were broke, nor hear because your hearing aid was not working properly and to top it off you could not move much in bed as you were connected to the ventilator.

Regardless of all this trauma you somehow still managed to communicate with your loved ones, nurses and consultants. Each day you became stronger and within a couple of days with a little help from mum's old glasses on you were ready to start writing words. The first words you wrote to mum and Lilly, "Where have you been all day?" made everyone laugh that day and we could slowly start to see glimpses of our old Papa coming back. After that you insisted on getting your hair cut like our Chris and again everyone thought you were joking but the next day Chris the nurse sat you on a chair and shaved it all off. Mum said you looked like 'Gandhi' especially with your dark framed glasses on! You were happy anyway and that's all that mattered, a small weight was lifted from your head and was allowing you to see the light out of ITU and into the HDU ward (not without ease however), you jumped onto another rollercoaster which brought you down a lot and then back up, your ng feed tube kept coming out and they struggled to get it back in. For almost a week you had no food or your normal medication including your restless leg medication so they ended up sedating you to keep you comfortable and calm as you were extremely irritable and distressed and not cooperating well with the nurses as a result of the tube being out.

This meant they couldn't really progress much with weaning you off the ventilator and not much physio was happening either. The rollercoaster was staying down and felt like it just wasn't going to move that week so was tough on everyone to see especially mum & Radha, as they were around and had to see you distressed.

On the 2nd March you turned a corner and slowly that rollercoaster started to move up again all because they finally managed to insert the ng tube back in the right position and could start giving you food and your normal medicines again. You started to become calmer again and responding, communicating with everyone. (Btw that week was also when storm 'Emma' met the 'Beast from the East' you will see a lot of photos on your phone of the blizzard we got as a result of the storm and about 2 ft of snow in Dublin and quite a lot in Pontyclun too from what I hear). That night Rahul left you with your headphones on listening to 'bhajans'. The next morning the nurses already could see a difference in you and felt you were back to 'the land of living'. We were so happy to hear this as it meant that you could start doing some lung exercises and breathing by yourself again without the ventilator support, and they did just that.

You were on a chair, a bike and doing sprints every hour i.e. breathing by yourself and getting stronger every minute. We were so proud of you and suddenly we were on a high.

On the 4th March they decided to move you to the HDU (high dependency unit next door). Immediately I thought this was a good thing as knew they wouldn't move you if they thought you were critical and that's what they said. You were still critical but not as critical as other patients coming into the ward.

You continued to improve over the coming days and your sprints became longer and longer everyday which was moving in the right direction finally. We were all on a high this week and I was glad to be coming back to Pontyclun with my boys, your grandsons Alex and Dylan (first time travelling by myself with them but needed to do this as I really wanted them to see you plus I didn't want to leave them behind again!).

On the 8th March our flight arrived in Cardiff at 10am with no delays or tantrums as all were well behaved and everything went to plan. That morning they decided to insert the speaking valve / tube in your throat to allow you to speak again and slowly you were able to converse with us all. We all came into see you that afternoon with Dylan and Alex and it was great to see you alert and chatting for the first time in 4 weeks. Again the nurses kept reassuring us that you were doing well with your coughing, breathing, eating solids and your strength... and slowly you started to become more independent with your mobility.

On Friday 9th March, it was Rahul's 29th birthday and we came into see you... you were looking great again after another good night sleep. The nurses mentioned that they may look to remove the trachi early next week because you were doing all the breathing by yourself at this stage... while me and Rahul were talking to you about that fact that you thought Rahul was getting married, you coughed so strongly that your trachi came out of your throat slightly and the consultants decided to take it out completely that day as they all agreed you were doing so well, and they weren't wrong, you continued to do well over the weekend and by Mothering Sunday 11th, Vicky our favourite nurse, decided to bring you down to the hospital canteen to meet us all for coffee and cake baked by Radha for Mother's day.

It was the most memorable and probably the best Mother's day for us all. You were there sitting with ALL your grandchildren and us (except Lilly, Rahul and Jij as they were in Dubai for Lilly's 40th) drinking coffee and eating cake just like the good old days and that's when we turned another corner, we left the hospital in high spirits that day and not just from the sugar rush. It was the *Papa rush*, all of us being there together as a family again!

On Monday morning 12th March, we got a phone call saying that the consultants had decided to discharge you to the normal ward 19 and that all the care you needed could be managed there with the small amount of O_2 you were on which they aim to reduce eventually (2 litres to 0) and physio to help you become more mobile over the coming days.

We were all a little anxious about the move to normal ward and not getting that 1 to 1 care but knew that was the only way out of the hospital and for you to prove to them that you could do this by yourself again. You were happy to move as well and could slowly see that light at Clos Springfield getting brighter with your guardian Angel calling once again.

Over the course of that week in ward 19 you started to hear properly again once your hearing aids were replaced and by Friday 16th you were on zero O_2, could stand / walk with help (mainly from your Angel by your side making sure you were getting stronger and were being looked after) and finally see and read again thanks to Radha who managed to get your optician to repair your glasses that were damaged in ward 6 before you went to ITU. You were starting to feel human again.

On Saturday 17th March (St Patrick's Day) Lilly, Rahul and Jij returned from their trip to Dubai and that night there was more snow on the way but this time not as bad as the 'beast from east'. The next day for the first time in nearly six weeks you sent your first text message to: "The Singh Diaries" and told everyone how well you were and not to come to hospital due to bad weather. We were so happy just to see you sending a normal text with actual sentences and full stops and by Monday 19th you sent us another message saying how you were getting more stable on your feet and that Dr Neale was happy to send you home that afternoon.

The day we had all been anxiously waiting for had finally arrived and the rollercoaster was coming to a stop. The helicopter (Chris's new car) arrived from London that afternoon and all of a sudden you were at home with your loved ones. I could see and talk to you on your phone again at home looking happy and relaxed. We were so happy to have you home for two nights at least but unfortunately the rollercoaster had to take you back to the hospital on the Wednesday 21st morning, you were coughing a lot and your breathing got worse again.

Nobody wanted to mention pneumonia again but it was at the top of everyone's list of worries. It did not make sense, not from the bloods and scan results, luckily this time it was fluid round the lungs and they gave you water tablets to remove this, once again they stabilised you with O_2 and nebulizer and you were well enough to be sent home on Friday 23rd and once again your rollercoaster stopped and the helicopter flew you home safely.

My Aerlingus plane flew me and Darragh to Lisbon for his 40th, I was happier going knowing that you were well again and the problem with fluid was fixed. It is now Monday 26th March and we are on the plane back to Dublin from Lisbon. We had an amazing couple of days on our own but were so looking forward to seeing my boys again and talking to you this evening! Just before I boarded the plane today I read that you finally got vaccinated against pneumonia, one of many vaccines we make at my Pfizer site in Dublin, protects you against thirteen common strains and hopefully this will prevent you to some extent against future infections, other preventions are keeping mobile, healthy and warm in the cold weather so here's to the start of your 2018 and a healthier new year!

Papa just one last thing... I can't stop wondering if only I had mentioned this vaccine to you before 2017 and if only the vaccination was on the list amongst others for over 65s in the UK that may be we wouldn't have gone on this rollercoaster ride or maybe we still would? We will never know I guess but there is a lesson to be learned from all this.

We are all so lucky to have you back Papa and blessed with a second chance to tell you how much we really appreciate you and all that you have done for us, love always,

Your daughter,

Neha

GOD WAS ON OUR SIDE

Prayers have power. If we pray with our body, mind and spirit in complete harmony, our prayers do not go unheard. They say, 'wherever mind goes the energy flows'. So, if our intentions are right and we put our minds to it, action is bound to follow, and the results are inevitable. As my daughter described, on Saturday 17 February 2018 at 2:30pm a very loud noise was heard and the whole hospital shook. Perhaps that event helped me wake up? It was revealed on the news that a magnitude 4.4 earthquake had struck with the epicentre north of Swansea.

Was that merely a coincidence? A meaningful coincidence? Or was God on our side?

Greg Braden, a great philosopher during his search for truth travelled far and wide, east to west and met various saints and sages who harboured miraculous powers of high mental activity. They ranged from traditional monks, from ancient Hindu scholars to the followers of the philosophy of Buddha to Islam, Judaism and various religions of the world. He has given an account of many miraculous incidences of high mental activity from removing a tumour from the stomach to making rain by chanting and praying. Our prayers do not go unheard, our thoughts have power which make things happen. He had a hobby of playing guitars and said that if we put two, properly tuned guitars on opposite ends of a room and plucked one string on one guitar, the same string on the other guitar would make a noise as if it had been plucked too.

The universe is a system of activity. We all are part of this system. 'We all', meaning the whole cosmos. Each cell in our body is interconnected with each other. And all the living organisms are interconnected with each other and with the whole system of the cosmos by a web of electromagnetic force. They are all in perfect harmony. Each cell in our body knows what other cells are doing. Each atom in the universe does not move without taking the entire cosmos with it. The power of this force has a common origin, perhaps the big bang some 13.7 billion years ago, which is vast and ever expanding? Extending beyond galaxies and stars, it has no boundaries. Endless, beyond our imagination. This web of energy is the field of unlimited possibilities also referred to as soul spirit or consciousness. Our life is a continuum of experiences of the moment now between birth and death. These experiences arise from and subside into this field of unlimited energy.

The experiences are the excitations created by our thoughts in the ocean of consciousness arising and subsiding as waves of energy. Each time a thought arises mind is created out of consciousness. Mind, then creates experience out of memories in its subconscious mind. If mind creates experience out of excitations, mind is also the source of union (yoga) with the soul through which quietening of the excitations of mind takes place. When connected to the common source of energy, the mind is in peace and harmony with the body and soul. All these come from a different dimension, which is non-local and of a higher state of mind, without any cause, without any attachment, no ego, nor karmic involvement. Just pure consciousness. Socially induced conditioning separates us from the rest of beings, the pure consciousness as described by Dr Deepak Chopra in his book, Synchrodestiny.

Intention is key. Our body is the sum of all our intentions, thoughts, feelings and emotions and so are our minds."

SATI SAVITRI

Despite many odds we made it out of the Royal Glamorgan Hospital. My entire family and I are very grateful to the NHS and the entire team who made it possible. Many were positive about my recovery but there were some who were negative and thought I was never going to make it. For them it was a miracle but for us – God was on our side.

I must not forget my angel wife who was always on my side fighting without fear with anybody if she thought that things were not going right in any way. I was unconscious but I could hear her loud and clear shouting in grief at nurses or the consultants until her voice was lost in the air. On one occasion she was really on her high horse when a consultant came to her and said, "He is not going to make it." She kept crying and shouting, "No!... No!... NO!" The consultant left as she stared at the door swinging back and forth... back and forth... back and forth behind him. She can't say for certain how long she stared at that door for.

Finally, the consultant came back through the door. His appearance had changed. He was tall...He was dark...He was fat...He had a big moustache... and He had a deadly weapon in his hand.

'I am YAMA DOOT (messenger from the kingdom of the dead), I have come here to take your husband,' he roared to her. 'OVER MY DEAD BODY,' my angel wife shouted without any sign of fear. 'I have looked after him all my life. He is mine. He is mine. You can't even touch him,' she declared.

Seeing her so determined the YAMA DOOTA said, 'I'm only a messenger, I will have to go back to the kingdom with what you have said.' He left with the door swinging back and forth... back and forth... back and forth...

Soon the door opens again and in enters the senior consultant. His appearance had changed too. He was tall... He was dark... He was fat... He had a big moustache... and He had a deadly weapon in his hand.

'I am YAMA RAAJ (The king of the dead). I have come here to take your husband with me,' he announced in his kingly voice. My Angel wife tactfully changed her tone. 'LONG LIVE THE YAMA RAAJ... LONG LIVE THE YAMA RAAJ... LONG LIVE THE YAMA RAAJ.'

She praised him again and again. Yama raaj was very pleased to hear her praises. But he said, 'I am here to get your husband to YAMA LOK (The kingdom of the dead) and it's my duty to do so. You knew and your parents knew that your husband was destined to die today. The palm reader told your father about it.'

'O Lord... O King of kindness. LONG LIVE THE YAMA RAAJ... LONG LIVE THE YAMA RAAJ... LONG LIVE THE YAMA RAAJ...'

My Angel wife kept praising him and said to him that she

was completely unaware of this. As she uttered these words, someone tapped on her back... who could hardly walk on his feet. Could hardly see or speak and said in his broken words, 'Yes my little baby, it's true. Please forgive me. Please forgive me. Because of this I lost all my land. I am living like a beggar and now you are losing your dear husband too. Since your marriage I kept praying to Lord Shiva for your long-married life. Please forgive me... please... please... please. It is all my fault.'

The YAMA RAAJ was listening to all this and became very sympathetic. He said, 'OK, here is a boon... you can ask for anything!'

'Give my father his health, his eyesight, his hearing and his strength back,' she said, before he could even think of changing his mind. 'SO, BE IT,' the YAMA RAAJ declared whilst raising his right hand.

'LONG LIVE THE YAMA RAAJ... LONG LIVE THE YAMA RAAJ... LONG LIVE THE YAMA RAAJ....'

My angel wife kept on praising him as he progressed towards me. 'But I love him so much... I can't live without him...' I can't live without him she kept pleading.

42

'I can give you another boon,' said the YAMA RAAJ. 'You can ask for anything!'

'Give my father all his land back she said without giving time to change his mind.' 'SO BE IT,' the YAMA RAAJ declared whilst raising his right hand. 'Now, I must take his soul. The YAMA RAAJ insisted.

'LONG LIVE THE YAMARAAJ... LONG LIVE THE YAMARAAJ... LONG LIVE THE YMARAAJ...' She kept praising on and on and on. 'Take my soul with you and let them burn my body to ashes along with his.'

The YAMARAAJ was getting irritated and annoyed by now. 'This is the final boon for you. You can ask for anything but let me take his soul.'

'Bless me with four beautiful children; three girls and a boy,' my Angel wife very cleverly asked. 'SO BE IT,' the YAMA RAAJ declared whilst raising his right hand and said in distraction, in his kingly voice...

'LONG LIVE THE YAMA RAAJ... LONG LIVE THE YAMA RAAJ... LONG LIVE THE YAMA RAAJ... 'But how can I have children without my husband?' my Angel wife asked with a smile of victory on her face.

'SO BE IT,' the YAMA RAAJ declared whilst raising his right hand for the last time before leaving the door swinging back and forth. Back and forth... back and forth...

The operation was successful.

The above story is based on a story from ancient India. The story is called 'SATI SAVITRI'. The strong bondage of love from a wife for her husband could be so powerful that even death could not separate her from her husband. At the death of the husband the wife used to burn herself along with the body of her husband so that the physical bodies can be destroyed and burnt into ashes, but the union of soul is forever and ever, age after age. They are called SATI.

Such a girl has special power so much so that her power of love can bring her husband back from even the hands of the God of death. SAVITRI was the daughter of a powerful king ASHWAPATI while SATYAWAAN was the son of a blind king who had lost his entire kingdom and was living in the jungle. SAVITRI fell in love with SATYAWAAN. She declared to marry him knowing that he was destined to die soon. Her father the King

Aswapati did not approve. But this made no difference. SAVITRI married SATYAWAAN and lived with her husband and blind father-in-law in the jungle. Finally the time came when SATYAWAAN was destined to die. But the power of love for SATYAWAAN not only brought him back from the kingdom of dead but also brought the lost eyesight and the lost kingdom for her father-in-law back too.

Even today, SATI SAVITRI is remembered during the festival of Karvachaut when women in India pray for their husbands' long life.

THE BODY, MIND AND SPIRIT

There are no boundaries to knowledge. Therefore, it is difficult to discuss the three topics separately. Today the people of different faiths and beliefs, the scientists of different disciplines, the theologians, the humanitarians and so on are willing to join in pursuit of a common goal for humanity... that we all are the system of the same and the same flows through us all. TAT TWAM ASI meaning 'Thou Art That' – preached thousands of years ago by the saints and sages of India. The traditional way of thinking is that there is a materialistic world in which this body is a part of, and in this body, there is a brain and mind is the biproduct of the brain. Professor Amit Goswami, a quantum physicist talks about upward causation and downward causation.

Upward causation is the traditional way of thinking as described above. The elementary particles form more and more complex particles to form unicellular organisms like Amoeba, where mind and brain are restricted to respond to stimuli like light, food etc. The multicellular organisms are a community of unicellular organisms which, over the years, undergoes further complicated evolutionary processes to form what is to be the human body with trillions of cells in complete harmony with a complex neural network, with the brain being part of it. And mind is the extension of the brain, which connects us all with consciousness and with the whole cosmos. But the problem is how the brain, which is made of matter, can communicate with the consciousness, which is non-material? The field of infinite possibilities?

Downward causation is the other way around. Mind being the biproduct of what is called consciousness in the field of unlimited possibilities and the whole world of objects in the entire cosmos including our body and brain in it, is the biproduct of the consciousness.

Quantum physics plays an important role in solving the problems. Elementary particles like electrons show a weird behaviour. They show a wave-like pattern like waves of energy however, at the same time, they also behave like particles of solid matter. This has been demonstrated by double slit experiments several times in recent years. The multiplicity and diversity of the objective world in the entire cosmos is the creation of our minds.... the sub conscious minds. There is no past. There is no future. Everything happens in the moment of now. Passage of time and space is an illusion created by the continuum of experiences by our subconscious minds moment by moment.

J. Krishnamurti suggests that for each experience there is an experiencer and the experienced. For each observation there is an observer and the observed. And when there is no time and space between them, observers become the observed, experiencer becomes the experienced. The time and the space collapse. All Is One.

Dr Deepak Chopra said, these solid materials are producing a construct created by human mind. A lot of research has been done on the functioning of the brain and how various parts of the brain respond to various experiences by the body. Actual electro-chemical substances initiate a biochemical response. Each and every bodily experience correlate in the brain, which then very cleverly edits and creates what is called reality in the mind. The consciousness.

The Double Slit Experiment; the elementary particles like electrons are the tiny particles of matter. They behave like tiny solid particles, quite understandably.

But they also behave like waves of energy, quite weird even for a physicist.

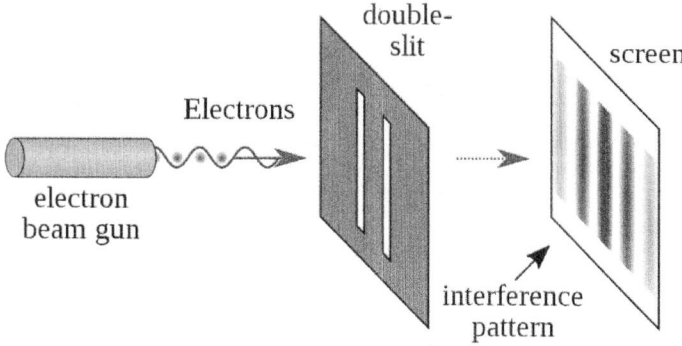

The above double slit experiment, which has been repeated several times in recent years by different scientists suggests that the simple act of observation by an independent observer collapses the wave function and the same electrons behave like solid particles.

As shown in the diagram, the tiny little electrons when shot through a slit randomly, form a straight line pattern on the screen behind. Similarly, when waves of water are forced through the slit, they form a straight line pattern on the screen behind. Quite understandably. But when the same experiment is repeated through double slits, the results were a bit different. The electrons form a pattern of two straight lines whereas the waves of water form a pattern of several lines, a pattern they call is an interference pattern. That is when the waves of water pass through the two slits they interfere with each other and hence the interference pattern on the screen behind. That's understandable too. Now, when the electrons are shot through the single slit randomly, the pattern is a single straight line as expected. But when the shots of electrons were fired through double slit, the pattern on the screen was that of interference pattern... a wave like function. Weird as it is, they decided to repeat this experiment. Electrons were fired again through double slits, but they decided to observe what happens when the electrons pass through the slits. The result was even more surprising. The pattern was that of two straight lines like that of solid particles concluding, therefore, that the simple act of observation by an independent observer collapses the wave function and the same electrons behave like solid particles.

THE BODY

The traditional methods of studying living organisms have long been suggestive of the fact that all living organisms are made of small units called cells. Each of these cells contain about 23,000 genes. Each of these genes are made of fundamental units... C, H, O and N to form Adenine, Thymine, Cytosine and Guanine.

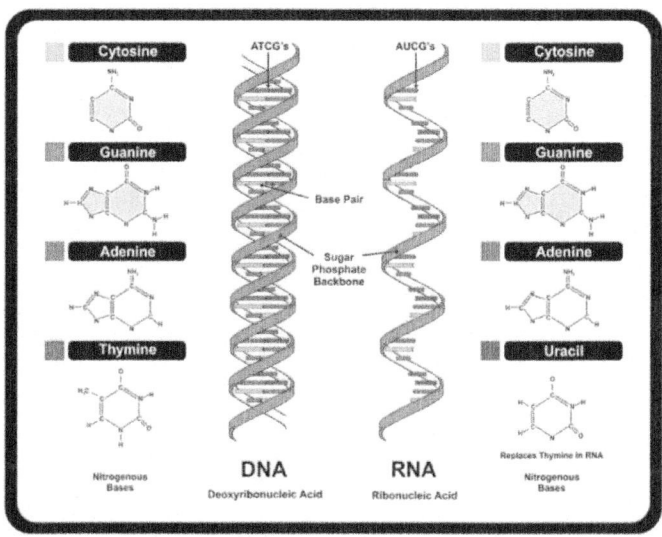

Adenine always paired with Thymine and Cytosine with Guanine to form a unique sequence of a double helix structure called DNA (Deoxyribose nucleic acid).

Lying within the three-letter genetic code like ATC or

GCT or AAA or CCA (A for adenine, T for thymine, G for guanine, C for Cytosine etc.) is the secret to our heredity, the fundamental basis of the chemistry of life; the sum total of all the information of data uniquely stored in our subconscious mind. Each and every cell in our body has the necessary intelligence and memory to reproduce itself.

The Three Areas of the Brain

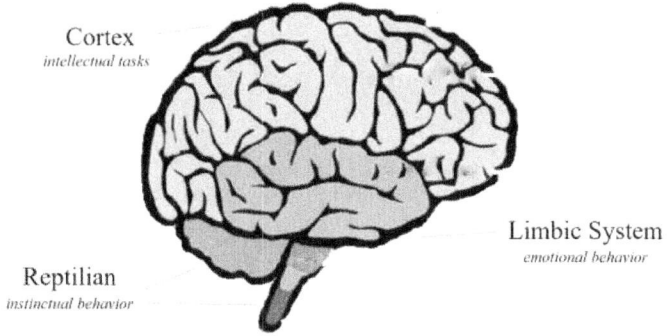

Cortex
intellectual tasks

Limbic System
emotional behavior

Reptilian
instinctual behavior

The development of the brain and its evolution over time played an important role in bringing human beings to the top of the evolutionary ladder. The part of the brain which separates us from the rest of the animal kingdom is the cerebral cortex from the limbic brain or reptilian brain. The reptilian brain is said to have evolved mainly for survival purposes whereas the cortical brain is much larger and has evolved us into a higher dimension of life. Thoughts. Feelings. Emotions. Love. Peace. Anger. Ego... and above all, it has the function of memory and the power of imagination. To some, this part of the brain is the main cause of all the sufferings of human kind today.

In fact our brain has enormous capabilities more than what we have learned to use. We experience the outside world through five senses... the seeing, touching, hearing, smelling and tasting. See how small my eyes are yet I can see the trees, the mountains, the dark starry sky. When Lord Krishna was a baby, he opened his mouth wide and everyone saw the whole universe in his mouth. You are not in the universe, the universe is in you, curving back into your experience, said the sages and saints of India over 5000 years ago.

A fertilised egg in the womb of mother carrying 23,000 genes from mother and the same number of genes from father multiplying until a fully-grown baby is born.

During this process, apart from cell division, the development of a baby can be said to undergo a number of miraculous stages. According to some, during the 3rd month of pregnancy a flurry of development of neural networks takes place. Some believe that the soul enters the body from the soul world during this time. Each cell in our body is intertwined and knows what other cells are doing. They are a self-organising, self-evolving and self-creating system.

THE MIND

Mind has no location and has no space or time. It is nowhere and it is everywhere, popping up and out of unlimited possibilities of consciousness. We can think of consciousness as being a vast lake without any boundaries in which mind rises and subsides as tiny ripples when a stone is dropped into it. Think of the stone as a metaphor for our thoughts. It is subject to our Karmic account and hence to life bondage.

It is unique to me yet part of the whole cosmos which itself is evolving. It is the bank of data and information in my subconscious mind passed on to me through my hereditary process. It is the intelligence of each cell in my body.

When I am driving a car, who, is the driver? Is it my arms and legs or my brain or there is a separate 'I' receiving instructions from my decision-making system of my mind... the intellect... consciously or subconsciously?

Recently I had operation on my right eye. Cataract removed and a new lens put in. All set. I was lying on the operation bed still and flat. The consultant kept reminding me that I must not move. Soon the eye was injected with local anaesthesia and I was ready for action. A sophisticated microscope hovered around my right eye as I looked at the consultant nervously who was busy chatting with her assistants about her broken washing machine, trying to find someone to repair it. As she was writing down some telephone numbers, I was becoming self-conscious about my stillness and the wheezing noise coming out of my throat, thinking that it was time for action.

She tapped my shoulder gently and declared, 'It's all done Mr Singh.' 'Did I hear all done? I questioned. 'Yes Mr Singh. All done.'

Who did the operation I wondered? Was it the consultant, her highly sophisticated machine or some kind of super mind?

A very common phrase is 'mind is the mistake of our intellect'. A thought arises in our consciousness, which has no feeling or emotions until it is analysed by the intellect through our system of preconditioned mind. A thought created in the mind stimulates a part of the brain initiating a biochemical activity, which then leads to appropriate action (karma).

Dr Bruce Lipton a famous biologist, working on stem cells came up with an idea of 'New Biology'. Stem cells are embryonic cells formed after a fertilised egg cell undergoes a repeated cell division. These stem cells are genetically identical. Yet when he grew these cells in different Petri dishes with different culture medium, meaning different environmental conditions, they produced different kinds of cells. He concludes, therefore, that it is not the genes, but it is the environment, which control the gene expression.

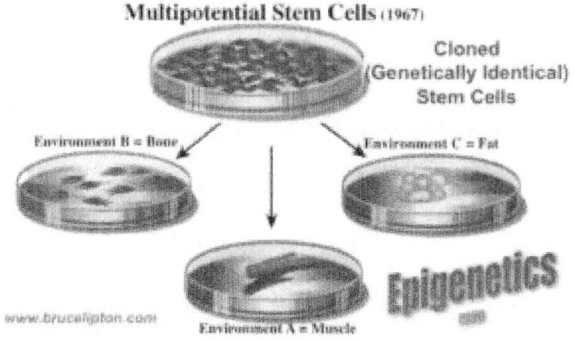

Multipotential Stem Cells (1967)

Cloned (Genetically Identical) Stem Cells

Environment B = Bone

Environment C = Fat

Environment A = Muscle

www.brucelipton.com

Epigenetics

We can think of the human body as being a community of trillions of cells, millions dying and reproduced every so often. Blood being the culture medium supplying necessary nutrients and hormones for the growth and repair of these cells. I can control the nutrients and hormones in the cells of my body by controlling what I eat and what I think. My mind's perception of the world can change my biology. So, if I can control my mind, I can control my biology. But the problem is that most of the time we run our lives with our subconscious mind, which is a conditioned mind.

When a child is born, during the first six years the child's mind is busy recording everything from all experiences around. All these experiences form the part of conditioned mind.

A thought created in mind stimulates a part of brain which then initiates a chain of reactions eventually supplying hormones through the blood. Different thoughts supplying different hormones at different state of minds... conscious or subconscious. Unfortunately, most of the time our thought process works through our subconscious mind independent of our conscious mind and hence it is subject to our past experiences, which form our conditioned mind, which is dominated mainly by negative thoughts.

Conscious mind, on the other hand, is creative and brings meaningful joy and richness to our lives by being mindful of all our actions.

I remember, the time after our marriage. Something had changed. I was thinking about her consciously all the time. Trying to look for every opportunity to talk to her or see her out of the crowd or touch her or even to be with her was a matter of great pleasure. My eyes were looking for her always. Consciously. The conditioned mind was hardly in picture. The afternoon in Delhi before I left India was extra special. It was an afternoon of the beginning of a relationship between our creative minds... a feeling of oneness.

THE SPIRIT

It was 1977. I had just joined my first teaching post in Nigeria in a place called Zaria. It was a residential institution and I oversaw a student's hostel. Ten o'clock in the night was the time for my routine inspection of the hostel. I left my angel wife in bed, half sleeping, jumped into my car and drove off. When I came back, I saw her in a terrible state. She was shivering and sweating and frightened. She jumped off the bed on to me. She saw her grandmother sitting next to her who died a few years back, she said. She had a high temperature throughout the night. First thing in the morning I took her to the doctor to find out that she was pregnant.

We were blessed with our first, beautiful little girl. If not all, most of us have experienced extra sensory perception. The concept of spirit is, perhaps, as old as the humanity itself. A human body is a community of about 60 trillion cells in perfect harmony. Each cell controls all the activities of itself at the same time aware of how the other cells are. Similarly, a community is a part of the broader community and eventually the whole cosmos.

By talking about 'spirit' we are talking about the field of energy, which connects us all. According to the ancient wisdom of India, the universe is made of five elements. They are Earth, Water, Air, Aakash and Fire. Another concept is Einstein's famous equation: $E = MC^2$. A pure scientific discovery, which joins together the spiritual concept of Shiva and Shakti, feminine vs masculine, zero vs one, possibility vs actuality, yin and yang. They all point towards the same conclusion; mass and energy are two sides of the same coin. The universe is governed by a cosmic duality.

When you introduce the modern-day weird concept of the quantum world where an electron behaves both like a solid particle and like energy, you can gain a clearer understanding of our journey through life. From the development of a baby in the womb, to the cradle, and then to the coffin. We have a community of 60 trillion cells in our body in perfect harmony with the rest of the cosmos, which connects our relationship with the soul world. We too, are mass and energy and our cosmic energies are observed in nature and beyond, connecting us to a world beyond our physical realm. Instead of the concept of cosmic duality, we can shift our thinking towards an understanding that we are all 'one' i.e. energy.

Bashar, (Born 12th October 1951, Ottawa, Canada) is a multidimensional being who for the past 35 years has claimed to channel a friend from the spirit world, Darryl Anka. Their relationship has hypothesised four basic laws of science:

1. Our existence is guaranteed. Once existed, you are always there. We change from one form to another.

2. One is all, and all is one. He created us all and He too, is the integral part of creation, holographically.

3. What we put out is what we get back. Physical reality is, in fact, a mirror reflection of what goes on within.

4. Change is the only thing, which is always constant.

It begs the questions, are genes always in control or are they only the carrier of hereditary information? Are the elementary particles a solid or a wave like energy?

The point I am trying to raise here, is simple. Are we ready for an organised system of evolutionary leap? A large quantum leap away from what we have been taught in textbooks? Are we ready for a tipping point or not yet? Or should we just wait for Lord Krishna himself? I can very well go to my local temple and ring the bell or to the church or to the mosque or to the Buddhist monastery at the foothills of the Himalayas and make my voice heard and shake the body, mind and the spirit of the whole cosmos and let Lord Shiva dance on the lightening tune of nature (The Prakriti) and say that we are awakened and ready. But are we really?

EVERYTHING IS ENERGY

When we see an object, believe it or not, it's only energy made up of various wavelengths, the solidity of the object is an illusion created by our own mind. A reflection of light energy from the object passes through the pupils of the eye and falls on the photoreceptor cells of the brain, which then takes part in photochemical reaction. The brain, then, through a chain of such reactions, interprets it as a picture in the retina, upside down.

The information stored in the subconscious mind help us perceive it as an object solid as it may look like a flower for example. Similarly, this path of perception doesn't follow the colour of the flower. The colour of the flower is also a creation of our subconscious mind.

When we hear a solid object fall to make a noise it's only a vibration, or vibrations in the air made up of certain frequencies, which, in turn, vibrate the tympanic membrane. The vibration then, passes through a set of three tiny bones, which connect to auditory nerves in the brain cells. Once again, the brain, with the help of the sub conscious mind perceives the sound.

When I am talking to you it may appear that the sounds are coming from my throat or lips or tongue. But no, they are only producing vibrations of different frequencies in the air, which again vibrate the tympanic membrane and a perception of sound is experienced in the subconscious mind through auditory nerves in the brain. Sensation of objects through touch, smell or taste work in a similar way.

The whole objective world is nothing but energy of different frequencies. The frequencies keep changing to give perception of different objects by our subconscious minds through our brain cells.

MEDITATION

Yes, everything is energy and I am excited about getting used to the idea that along with my mind and spirit, the layer of skin surrounding my body is not much of a barrier, rather it's also a medium through which my eternal self flows out and vice versa. That the breath in is a continuum of the same energy flow of the entire cosmos. That the electromagnetic field around my body... my aura, is a system of the same. Thinking about it, I have been living this energy all my life.

Meditation is as old as humanity itself. It's our way of life. Very much an individual way of life. We all must have noticed people on the streets of London, Delhi or Paris, all across the globe chanting 'HARE RAMA HARE KRISHNA'. Seen people praying with their eyes closed in front of various images and sculptures... in the caves... on the mountains... in the jungles... in the woods surrounded by nature... by the hospital bed holding the hands of loved ones in deep thoughts... offering prayers to their respective religious faiths Regardless of which religion, this form of meditation has for thousands of years connected humans to God, spirit, hope and to an unnamed energy beyond our physical form. The starry moonlit sky at the end of a busy day in London, or stretching your vision far beyond the sea's horizon. They are all webs of energy trying to squeeze into me or disperse out of me and yet they maintain a balance of universal energetics.

During the early years of my childhood I spent time in a small village with my grandparents along with inherent 36 crores Gods and Goddesses from Treta yuga with their aura constantly reminding me of good moral values. It was very much a joint family but everyone had a role to play and in that role: 36 crores Gods and Goddesses were never a crowd.

One of my aunts was responsible for making food for everyone... and I mean, everyone. Her morning would start with a bath and then prayers to as many Gods and Goddesses she could remember. The first few grains of rice must be offered to God, she must remember that, my grandmother told her that she should also remember to feed the first chapati to the cow and my grandfather never forgot to leave some food on his plate for the dog waiting outside. My elder grandfather whose legs were both amputated following an armed robbery, in his seventies, kept chanting mantras all day long. We had strict instruction to spend some time with him and talk to him.

In the midst of all this I had to keep an eye on a shadow created by a stick. I had to leave for my first day at school when the shadow reached a mark on the ground. A two-mile journey I must do everyday from now on... Goddess Sarashwati... the Goddess of learning. All I had to do was touch the chalk or draw a straight line to get a blessing from Goddess Saraswati and from my Guru ji. I touched his feet every morning I went to his school. He was from upper caste Brahmin and there was something special in him, I must say. He was tall and white with a string of long hair at the back of his head. There was some kind of radiant energy, I can't help feeling striking right into the pupils of my eyes and a general feel good factor in his presence. I didn't know then, but I know now. It was his aura. Monday to Friday and the Saturday was no holiday... rather a special day of prayers and rituals to give thanks. No books. Just a flower, some grains of rice, fruit and vegetables were all that was needed for the rituals. The whole place needed to be cleaned with cow dung. It was a good experience handling the cow dung with my own hands.

Left over cow dung was used for burning fire during the week for our Guru ji. Homework... I forgot about it. Must do every evening or in the morning before I left for school. In the name of science and technology, all we had was a lantern and kerosene oil. But do not forget the gaze of the 36 crores of divine souls which were also always present.

I was good in maths and reading and writing. But to be good was not always in my favour. For others 3 out of 10 marks was enough to escape punishment but for me it was 7 out of 10. And the punishment was harsh. I had to hold my two ears with both hands bending like a chicken. I did learn a lot, I must say. I still remember my times tables. It did not finish at 12×12. It was further complicated by 1 and a quarter times tables. Followed by 1 and a half and 2 and a quarter and so on. It went on and on for a year or two. At the end of the year came another set of rituals.

Every pupil would get an opportunity to visit their parents or grandparents in their villages with Guru ji during Guru Dakshina. Again, all that was needed for this ritual were grains of rice, food and flowers as well as blessings from Guru ji, our elders and of course the gaze of 36 crores deities. Over the years, I came to know them all off by heart. No one taught them to me, I just remembered them because I lived with them day in, day out. Not all of them made sense to me. I was frightened of seeing poisonous snakes even though we worshipped them at the same time.

The cobra dwells around the neck of Lord Shiva. My grandmother would tell me a bedtime story of how the deities and devils joined together pulling and pushing the ocean, churning it into a swell of water. A large mountain was tied by a huge serpent. As they churned the sea, a large amount of amrit (a potion granting immortality) was produced as well as a small amount of poison. Everyone wanted the amrit. But what about the poison? Lord Shiva swallowed it and stored it in his throat. Since then, his throat became permanently indigo in colour.

During the time of these stories being told to me, I was aligning my vortex to the power points (Chakras) in my body for a union (yoga) with the supreme soul. Until one day my father, mother and younger brother came to the village I was staying in. It became apparent that they were from a different world. My younger brother knew the science behind why the wind was stronger in hot weather. I didn't have a clue. He knew what happened to clouds in the sky. What lightening was. He knew why we hear thunder after lightening. I had no idea. He had all the answers. Our different schools of teaching meant that we had been taught vastly different skills. All praise and clapping for him was well deserved. Whereas my knowledge was based on stories of deities and devils and snakes. I felt inferior.

I went for a walk. Sat down under the huge bunyan tree by the pond with thousands of coloured threads hanging down from the branches. I felt like I was really stupid. A gang of boys came and poured dust and soil over me and went on and on laughing and giggling at me until someone elderly intervened. I felt like climbing up the tree and jumping off to kill myself, 'GO TO HELL,' I shouted in desperation. Which kept echoing in my mind, go to hell, go to hell... may be 36 crore times if I can remember correctly. Suddenly everything I did, the way I spoke, dressed, used my usual twig of neem tree to brush my teeth, ate my morning breakfast, my running around bare footed in the woods, playing games by climbing the tree and jumping off or even some of the yogic exercises my Guru ji taught me, became an act of stupidity and I was labelled as an idiot. The reality of how different I had become from the rest of my family was obvious.

Despite all of this I cannot forget my Guru ji. He may have looked funny with his long ponytail at the back of his head to my siblings but the energy, which radiated from his forehead, I can never ever forget. Not that it would make any difference. I was to live with my mother, father and other brothers and sisters from that point onwards.

New school, new teachers, new sets of rules and regulations... I was more interested in the air pressure of the kerosene stove, which made cooking or making tea much quicker. Fresh water from the tube well was a luxury for me. And of course, the extra care and affection from my mum and dad as well as my brothers and sisters that I missed out on. Slowly and steadily the feel-good factor from living with my own parents and brothers and sisters helped me to settle nicely into this new life.

However, I couldn't help feeling uneasy about my aura,

my vortex and about my chakras, and of course, the 36 crores of deities which I had previously developed close connections to. I couldn't fit these parts of my life into my new "modern" life.

For some unknown reason I became a quiet person. Call me an introvert. I became that. It became my personality. In my school days and in my later life. Maybe there is some connection between me being stupid or introverted and being influenced by the deities on the horizon? It's about judging people. It's about labelling others by imposing your own values. It's about value. It's about cultivating value through meditation. This is something I was always interested in practicing but was never successful.

There are many different types of meditation described by many. To mention the following four types may put things into perspective from my point of view.

1.   BHAKTI YOGA
2.   KARMA YOGA
3.   GYAN YOGA
4.   RAJ YOGA

These are the four different paths of yoga through which

mankind has been practicing union with the supreme world, the spirit world, the soul world and the consciousness since the existence of creation. By doing so we are bringing the electromagnetic force of our aura in alignment with various energy systems of the body, which then are channelled through the complex nervous system and then finally tuned to the entire cosmos. They are all energy of different frequencies. They all start with thoughts, feelings, emotions and experiences through various sensory and extrasensory perceptions.

Bhakti yoga is the union through love and devotion. To surrender a complete surrender. Like a drop of water falling from the sky knows nothing but to surrender to the vastness of the sea.

Karma yoga, similarly is the union through our good karma. Every karma has its effects and every effect has a cause. Every action has a reaction. It is our karma which creates bondage for birth and rebirth and we keep coming back generation after generation to settle our karmic account while the physical body gets recycled with the physical world.

Gyan yoga, on the other hand, is the union with God through knowledge. Knowing the truth and attaining wisdom through meditation. Love, peace, beauty, purity and power is my true nature. My ultimate destiny is to return back to these values.

Raj yoga is the control over our mind. Often we do things subconsciously. It's our sanskara being in control of what we do. It's about practicing to do things with our conscious minds.

SELF REALIZATION / SELF AWAKENING

I am a soul. I am a pure soul. I am a powerful soul. Love, Peace, Beauty and Truth is my original nature.

Through my body and mind I create thoughts and feelings and emotions. These create disturbance of peace of my mind. I am the creator of the disturbance of peace of my mind.

I am the pure consciousness, which shines on everything illuminating the world around. The world around is a mirror reflection of the world within. This is experience only as perceived through my mind.

I am a soul. I am a pure soul. I am a powerful soul. Love, Peace, Beauty and Truth is my original nature.

And so is the soul of all human beings. Big or small, rich or poor, able or disabled, men, women or children, black, white or brown.

This world is a stage and we all are souls in different costumes playing our role in the world drama. Each scene of the drama is perfect. Our journey from cradle to coffin and then coffin to cradle is cyclical. Linearity is an illusion created by our perceptual interpretation of its experiences in time and space.

One of the most commonly observable cycles is our life cycle itself. We are born. Then we grow up to a child. A child grows up to an adult. An adult, after marrying a compatible partner, takes up a great responsibility of reproducing a child or children and raises them into the adult stage. This then leads to the old stage. When our body slowly degenerates and then comes to the final stage when, one by one all the organs of our body fails to work. Heart stops. Brain stops. And the final stage comes what we call DEATH. At death we destroy the body... EARTH TO EARTH... SOUL TO SOUL. Yes, it is all ENERGY in the end.

Life in the organic world from amoebas to human beings, from microbes to plants, are all in cyclical order. So is the inorganic world of chemicals of the entire non biological cosmos. The energy produced during the 'Big Bang' and its aftermath of action and reaction is unimaginable to comprehend by the human race. Perhaps a self-organising, self-evolving universe, or even multiverse, is easier to understand. But what is beyond the 'Big Bang' is a mystery or perhaps there is an intelligence behind all of this, which is always present and is beyond the cycle of birth and death.

It could be said that there has always been something acting as an independent observer, which is indestructible.

Nainam chhindanti shastrani.

Nainam dahati pawakah.

Na chaiman kledyantyapo.

Na shoshyati marutah.

Weapons cannot cut it, fire cannot burn it, water cannot wet it, air cannot blow it preached by Lord Krishna over 5000 years ago in Mahabharata.

So, there is a cycle, and there is another cycle and there is another one and another... even bigger one... all entangled with each other in such a way that it never ends because there is something always there to carry forward to re start the cycle again and again.

This reminds me of a game I used to play with my friends in my childhood... And the game is something like this:

You think of an amount of money in your mind to start a business. Then borrow the same amount from your banker. I give you one hundred pounds from my pocket. Now total them all up. To start a business, you need blessings from Goddess Lakshmi. Pooja ceremony costs about half of the money raised. Now you realise that the amount of money you are left with is not enough to start the business. This meant you had to return all the borrowed money back. Of course, you returned the money back to the bank you borrowed it from.

The interesting part of the game is that I know that you have only fifty pounds left with you. You are amused to know that I knew. I remind you that I gave you one hundred pounds, meaning a shortfall of fifty pounds. These fifty pounds goes back into the bondage, which keeps the cycle going. You have to come back to settle the bill. Unless you settle the bill, the amount in the bill keeps adjusting life after life until the final day of liberation or MOKSHA... THE DAY OF COMPLETE FREEDOM. FREE FROM ALL KARMIC BONDS. FREE FROM THE CYCLE OF BIRTH AND DEATH.

CYCLE OF TIME AND REINCARNATION OF SOUL

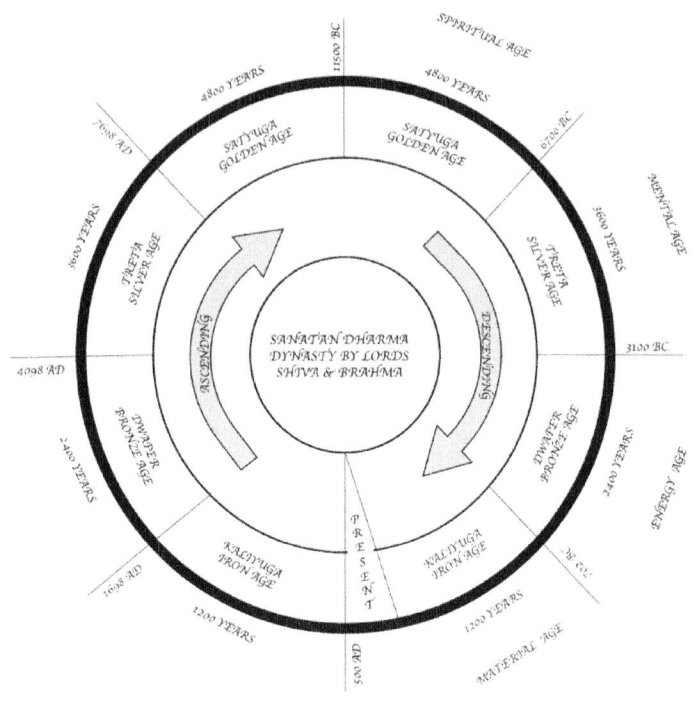

Presuming that 'Big Bang' is the beginning, which creates the system of the universe, then maybe the big bang itself is a cyclical process, which created the system of the universe with stars and galaxies and planets expanding due to energy produced by the big bang. This energy pushing the galaxies beyond the edge into the unknowable. Maybe it created further big bangs into the unknowable? The concept of multiverse therefore, is not beyond our imagination.

I think, I am going beyond my limitations. Let us talk about our 'little universe'... yes little universe because if we think of the whole cosmos, it's really... really... vast... unimaginably vast.

The distance between the Earth and the observable edge of the universe is about 46 billion light-years (1 light-year = 5.879×10 to the power 12 miles.) The distance travelled by light in one year = 300,000 km per second.

The universe perhaps, extends beyond our observable universe. This includes the entire space and time and everything in it. The planets the stars, the galaxies and all other forms of matter and energy. It is widely believed that there are about 100 billion galaxies in the universe. A galaxy has millions of stars. Our sun is just one of at least 100 billion stars in our milky way (galaxy) alone.

Then there is a question of dark matter and dark energy. The matter as we see is only 5% of the total existence. The sun, the moon, the planets, the galaxies, and anything or everything we see, touch, taste, hear or smell, belongs only to this 5%. Of the rest; 25% is the dark matter and remaining 70% is dark energy which does not react or reflect to the observable universe and is invisible.

The 5% matter as we experience it, is made of electrons, protons, and neutrons. Electrons and protons are -ve and +ve charged particles respectively orbiting round the nucleus containing neutrons. In between the particles there are empty spaces. These empty spaces play a significant role in the material world. It is said that if we take out all the spaces from one of the tallest buildings, the matter remaining will be equivalent to a grain of rice. Yes (less than 1% of the 5)... a grain of rice.

This reminds me of a tiny little seed. The tiny little seed has a great potential of, given the right environmental conditions, giving rise to a huge tree with its lovely green branches and leaves and flowers and of course seeds in large quantities and the cycle continues.

It is important to note that time has no beginning and no end and so the space is infinite and has no edge. Meaning the present is the start of the existing cycle. And therefore, there are parallel verses of different cycles. Perhaps these multiverses, each takes birth from chaos, grows, decays and dies into chaos. The famous law of entropy states that, 'things move from a state of perfection to a state of chaos'. A higher source, then, intervenes to take it back to perfection.

Souls are in a state of perfection in soul world. Though even in the soul world the souls are in different cycles of perfection moving from one level to another. From there we come in the world stage. Still as a perfect soul. This is Satyuga or Golden Age. In the cyclic order of time SATYUGA leads to TRETA. Deities and prophets were the divine souls who existed in this age. The population of pure and perfect souls in satyuga was about 9,000,000. Whereas by the end of Treta there were 36 crores (36,000,0000) deities. They were souls empowered with love, peace and happiness in perfect harmony. Afterwards, signs of duality creep in and attachment of the soul with the body starts, leading to lust, greed, anger and ego.

YADA YADA HI DHARMASHYA,

GLANIRVAWATAHBHARATAH

ABHYUTHANAM ADHARMASHYA

TADATMANAM SRIJAMYAHAM

PARITRANAAY SADHUNAAM

VINAASHAAY CH DUSHKRITAAM

PANAARTHAAY

SAMBHAVAANI YUGE YUGE

A quote from Geeta spoken by The Lord Krishna in the battle of MAHABHARATA some 5000 years ago.

Meaning:

Whenever, there is decline in righteousness and an increase in sinfulness. O Arjuna, at that time, I manifest on earth.... to protect the righteous, to annihilate the wicked, and to re-establish the principles of dharma, I appear on this earth age after age.

During the Dwaper age, pure souls like, the Prophet Mohammed, Jesus Christ, Buddha, Shankaracharya and Mahavir descended from the soul world to this world to give the message of one God to humanity. The scriptures were written to give powerful messages about values. These scriptures were to demonstrate war between deities and devils to give a message of victory of truth over evil.

We are in Kalyuga now. The devil elements of the society at its peak. Evident today as increasing violence, terrorism, global warming, socioeconomic injustice and so on. Perhaps it is time for HIM to reappear or perhaps he is already there.

So, the big bang itself is a cyclical process, which created the system of the universe with stars and galaxies and planets expanding due to energy produced by the big bang. This energy pushing the galaxies beyond the edge into the unknowable. As previously said, maybe it created further big bangs into the unknowable?

This brings us back to the question of our real-life experience. The cycle of death, birth and rebirth. The cycle of our karmic account. The cycle of the Soul world. The cycle of the physical world. There is a soul. The pure soul... the powerful soul. In complete harmony with love and peace... peace at last... THE SATYUGA.

BURDEN ON MY SHOULDERS

Rain or shine, wind or calm, cold or warm, I always see through my living room window, a postman passing, smiling and whistling with a heavy bag on his shoulder every morning. I take every opportunity possible to open my door and greet him good morning with a smile. I wonder, by the time he reaches back to his office how many people he leaves behind, happy or angry or distressed or even in tears. Same again next morning, I see the same postman with a heavy bag on his shoulder passing my living room window smiling and whistling. I wonder by the time he reaches back to his office, how many people he leaves behind happy or angry or distressed or even in tears.

As Christmas approaches, I see the same postman passing my living room window morning after morning. But his bag is getting heavier and heavier. His smile is restricted to greetings only and his whistling almost lost in his thick woollen scarf around his neck. He looks grumpy tired and exhausted. I felt like opening the door and offering him a cup of tea or coffee. But I thought I better not. He is on a mission today to make many people happy with Christmas cards and gifts.

I imagine, many people like me, old or young, men women or children watching the same postman passing their windows and running up to the door in excitement only to find a bare doormat and a cold winter chill howling through their letterbox. Once again I wonder by the time he reaches back to his office how many people he leaves behind, happy, angry, distressed or even in tears.

Christmas is over and the same postman is back in the street again carrying the bag on his shoulder, smiling and whistling without realising that he is still carrying it on his shoulder. Nothing has changed. I still wonder by the time he reaches back to his office, how many people he leaves behind, happy angry distressed or even in tears.

I look within myself and realise l am no different. I, too, am carrying a heavy bag. I too, am carrying a burden without realising it... The burden of my Karma.

KARMA

Karma is our action. What we do. What we speak. What we think.

Thought is the faculty of our mind and so is our intellect. Our thoughts filter through intellect and creates a feeling. Feeling creates attitude and then an action is performed. Repeated actions create habits. These habits become engraved in our subconscious mind as our belief system. The sum of these habits become our sanskar.

In any action, most of the time it's our subconscious mind which is in operation not our conscious mind. Like driving a car. We can drive a car for miles without thinking consciously about it.

'Every action has equal and opposite reaction.' It's a widely accepted scientific understanding. Similarly, 'As you sow so you reap', is a widely known religious belief.

We reap the fruits of our own karma. Karma can also be explained by the principle of cause and effect. Every cause has an effect and every effect has a cause. What we are today, our achievements, both physical and non-physical, is a result of the reactions of our past actions and what we will be tomorrow will depend on the fruits of our karma today. That's our destiny. Our karma today determines our destiny tomorrow. How and when is a big question though.

Is there an independent witness somewhere who is keeping a balance sheet of all our karmic accounts? Is the law of karma purely a physical phenomenon and is governed by physical law like the law of chemistry or the law of physics or is it something metaphysical?

A saint while crossing a river comes across a scorpion who is drowning. Out of pity the saint picks up the scorpion. The scorpion out of habit stings the saint. The saint as a reflex action drops the scorpion back in the water. The scorpion is drowning again. The saint picks it up again. The scorpion stings again. This goes on and on until the saint and the scorpion both are ashore. This can be a good analogy of karma and destiny. The saint being stung by the scorpion is his destiny, the effect of his past karma, and the act of the saint saving the scorpion from drowning in the river is his karma which yield fruits in the future. But then maybe it's not as simple as this.

A little village girl lights up her lantern to do her homework. Soon the glass of the lantern gets covered by smoke and it's too dark to read or write. The poor girl is the victim of the karma of the kerosene oil manufacturing company. Some people are born with a silver spoon in their mouths while the other suffers from malnutrition. Today we all know the benefits of science and technology. But we are also aware of global warming, pollution and its role in our lives, war, terrorism and many other socioeconomical effects of science and technology.

Imagine a little girl of 7 years old, while running around in school, collides with a bench and hurts herself badly. She was crying. She was bleeding from her knee. Nobody was around and she was looking for someone. One of her friends passing by noticed. She picked her up. Helped her by taking her to the head teacher where she was bandaged. The teacher was sympathetic and asked her if she wanted to go home. She declined and continued with her classwork. 'It is painful but I will manage,' she said to herself. School closed and she went home. Her mother asked what had happened, to which she replied, 'I fell in the school. It's painful but I will manage,' she said.

'I am going to Tesco, tell your father when he comes home. You might need to go to hospital,' says her mother. She rushed off to Tesco where she worked part time every evening. It was pointless waiting for dad as she knew for sure that he must have gone to the local pub with his friends for a pint. As usual she went to school the next morning. Her teacher asked. Her friend asked. 'It's OK,' she said. 'It's still hurting but I will manage,' she said to herself.

Slowly the bandage got blown away by the strong wind and the wound got healed naturally. There was no pain. The mark on the knee, you can hardly notice. It's a year since then. She has moved to upper class now but passing through the corridor she always remembers that classroom. There is no visible wound. There is no visible scar. But the scar in her mind is always there. That scar always reminds her of the rise and fall of various hormones which she had to go through. As she fell, she thought that the whole world was falling apart and when she saw the blood, she thought she was going to die, she was frightened. And she can't forget the much needed compassionate touch from her friend and sympathetic words from her head teacher. Also the neglectful and no care attitude from her parents. Each of these behaviours stimulated a specific part of the brain to produce specific hormones to have a specific imprint on her mind. If this world is a stage and we all are playing our roles in different costumes on this world drama, the script of the scene is perfectly written according to karmic account. Each of these are the perfect reflections of cause and effects to our karmic accounts.

It appears that in this game of cause and effect or action and reaction or karma and destiny we are all together intricately joined with each other in a web of energy. Our feelings and emotions, our pain and sufferings, our sorrow and happiness, they are all interconnected in this web of energy.

All actions start with a thought. Like graviton is a unit of gravity, photon is a unit of light, thought is a unit of action. Action and reaction, cause and effect, karma and its fruits, are all physical phenomena, which are guided by the physical laws like the laws of chemistry or the laws of physics and therefore can be proved or disproved by science. A thought is non-physical in nature and has no physical properties. It is wave-like metaphysical energy, which is non-local and has no time and space. Someone asked me a question.

'What was the best day of my life when I was 18 years of age?' With a little effort I could remember it, remember it in minute details. We all can do it. The point is where was this information until then? The answer is consciousness or awareness, which is a field of unlimited possibilities and contains all the information.

A great philosopher Rupert Spira has defined consciousness as in which all the experiences appear. It is that with which all experiences are known. And it is that out of which all experiences are made. Experience meaning any objective experience like thoughts, concepts, feelings, sensations, ideas, memories, sights, sounds, tastes, smells textures etc. All of these appear in consciousness or awareness.

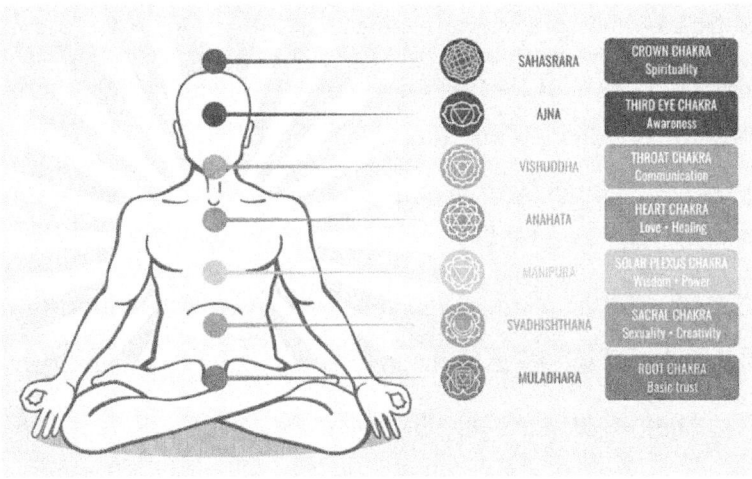

Scientists today know a lot more about our brain and how it functions. But when comes to thoughts, feelings and emotions, memories and sight, sound, touch, taste and smell - the field of consciousness - not many, but some, quite understandably, are willing to cross the ethics of science. However, in recent years there are many who have tried to help understand the nature and mechanics of consciousness and bridge the gap between science and spirituality and by doing so brought the scientists and non-scientists and the wisdom of the saints and sages of the past around the same table.

The brain is purely a physical structure. A highly complicated processor through which all our thoughts, feelings, emotions, perceptions and all our experiences filter through to create a complex chain of actions and reactions - chemical, physical and metaphysical in order to perform our karma our destiny. Thoughts come and go.

According to Rupert Spira each time a thought appears the mind comes into being out of the consciousness temporarily and then dissolves back into the unlimited field of consciousnesses as the thought disappears. This metaphysical phenomenon can also be referred to as 'Individual Units of Consciousness' as mentioned by Thomas Campbell, a well-known Nasa physicist in his famous book 'My Big TOE'.

We have all experienced the power of mind and its effects on our body. Pleasant and unpleasant thoughts create a bodily reaction such as heart beat, breathing, release of sweat and tears and so on. When we suck a real lemon our taste buds, salivary glands and certain parts of the body react in certain ways. The important point is that the same physical reactions can subsequently be prompted merely by the thought of sucking a lemon.

Religious and spiritual beliefs are vital to many people. Prayer and meditation help increase people's emotional wellbeing. It is known that people experience the relaxation response when they pray or meditate. Their blood pressure, heart rate, and levels of stress hormones drop. At the same time, the brain waves associated with relaxation increase. These physiological changes reduce anxiety and increase blood protein levels in the body indicating healthier immune system.

In the quest of body and mind the understanding of the biochemistry of thoughts and feelings can prove to be important for us.

There is no such thing as 'separate self'. Our consciousness is intricately linked with each other. Our personality is a result of interactions and behaviours with each other. The exchange of feelings and emotions like love and compassion modify the neuropeptide bonds in the brain, which create an increase in hormones like oxytocin, dopamine, serotonin and opiates in the brain.

These are the 'happy hormones', which are known as immunomodulators. Many scientists today, believe that biochemical reactions to all mental and emotional stimuli affect your everyday thoughts and feelings. These reactions do not only occur in the brain, but also simultaneously, in virtually every system of our body and every cell in our body. Karma isn't exclusive to the saying of 'what goes around, comes around' – it is wider than that. What and how you think affects your cells, which affects your body, which affects your behaviour which in turn, affects how you treat others, this then sets a chain of events as your actions affect the same trigger points in another person and the cycle continues.

The mechanisms by which experience, thoughts and emotions are translated into chemical expressions and then how this information is communicated through and subsequently affects our various biological systems will perhaps be the subject of scientific research of wide interest for years to come.

LIVING WITH DEVILS OF KALYUGA

Living with the devils in Kalyuga. To many, Hinduism is a way of life rather than an organised system of religion. As a Hindu my body, my mind and my spirit are shaped by my way of living. In ancient days when a child was born, during their early part of development, he or she would spend time with their family, friends and the nature around them, learning and familiarising themselves with the very beginnings of life lessons and connections.

Then when the children were a little older, they were sent to the jungle to spend time with the yogic Gurus. The first lesson was their connection with God. And with that first lesson they would learn the nature of the whole cosmos at a different level of understanding. The various laws of physics, chemistry or biology were taught through the ever-evolving body, mind and spirit. Their excellence was decided by their Gurus and they would repay their Gurus in dakshina i.e. payment in kind, respect and thanks. And then came adulthood. When they would perform their duty towards society in general. Have a family life. Be a good mother or good father. Teach the younger generation good values – good

Dharma. And finally, old age would set in. And their physical body would slowly stop working. This life cycle would go on and on, year after year, age after age... from Satyuga to Treta. From Treta to Dwaper. And from Dwaper to Kalyuga.

Much of the ancient life cycle still exists today. However, of course, our soul has lost its original value of unlimited, unconditional love, peace and happiness. 'I' and 'you' have become separated. Our physicality became separated from our soul. 'I' has shifted our identity to material identity. Duality eventually settled and greed crept in. Ego and anger followed, and we often surrendered our true values.

This is Kalyuga and I am fighting back my devil year by year... hour by hour... minute by minute. During the time when I was in intensive care for more than a month, I suffered from repeated pneumonia and three cardiac arrests. Each time I was resuscitated successfully thanks to the medical team. After recovery and as I was coming out, the doctors reminded me about the cardiac arrests and said to me that I may not make it through these doors next time.

This is kalyuga and once again I am at the mercy of the devils. The yamadoota. Fighting my own battle day by day, hour by hour, minute by minute. With the devils of kalyuga.

Not only do I fight them, but I also live with them like microorganisms, millions in my body. Don't worry, one day our body will learn to fight this new coronavirus and to live with it too.

The devil of Kalyuga is everywhere. It is in me, in you, in water, in air, in soil, in trees, in mountains. In the sun, in the moon, spread all over the place... in the entire cosmos. It comes in different forms, from tsunamis to floods. From volcanos to earthquakes. From global warming to various types of pollution. From religion to religion... From pockets of small ideologies to well established philosophies causing war across the world pushing the whole world into one unjust society. These are only some of the devils of Kalyuga. These are everywhere; large and visible or small and invisible.

I am fortunate enough to be born in independent India. I did study the history of the Moghal Kingdom in early school days. But only had a vague idea about the British

Raj in India and across the world and about the movement for independent India and the atrocities associated with it.

I was happy to leave India for the UK in 1971 to further my studies and look for a better career. After my MSc. degree, I with my wife Anju, went to Nigeria for teaching positions. We enjoyed the kind of life we had in Nigeria. Developed some friends, parties and picnics and get togethers after fulfilling my contractual agreements to the employer. My time in the UK and Nigeria also gave me an opportunity to meet different people with different experiences.

I saw the film 'Gandhi' for the first time. This had a great influence on me. I watched the famous film 'Roots', a film about black slaves. I was surprised to see what went on. I learnt about the holocaust... learnt about the Americans dropping the atomic bomb on Japan... learnt about evacuees where large numbers of small children were moved from their parents to a secret place during world wars. I realised that I was learning to live with the devils of kalyuga every day. We were happy to come back to the UK to settle finally. My main reason for doing so was to give my children a good education and a good career. And that's what we did.

My wife and I made sure that there was a roof over our heads and food on our tables and at the same time our children could achieve whatever they wanted to achieve. Being involved in running a post office and a grocery business, it gave me an opportunity to meet people in the local community of various needs. I couldn't help being observant of the people around me from different vulnerable groups.... due to their age, socioeconomical injustices as we all were learning to fight and live with the devils of kalyuga.

Being an immigrant, it was even more difficult for us. I could see in the eyes of my children almost every evening after school and in the depressed mood of my wife after she closed the shop. But we went on. Had no other choice.

One day I decided to go to a local pub for a drink. I saw a bunch of people with familiar faces. I joined them. Had a good couple of hours with them. Then I left. It was a good start, I thought. I decided to have another go. As I approached, I saw through the window the same group of people. I was going to join them. As I was buying a drink for myself one of the men from the group approached me and kept chatting to me and made sure I do not join them. It was not funny but true. I never went back to that pub after that apart from occasionally with my family.

In another experience, one late evening around 10.30pm a middle-aged woman knocked the door. She was drunk and she wanted to buy a bottle of gin. We knew the woman. She was local and came walking. Maybe she couldn't drive in her state. I called my wife and decided to sell her the gin on the condition that we drop her at her house in our car. She agreed and so we did. It was a huge farm house. She then started to make a habit of it until one evening I refused. A few doors away from our post office a man used to live on his own. Youngish, sober and well behaved always. He used to work in the mines and on his way back from work he used to withdraw cash from the post office and then buy a bottle of whisky along with other things from the shop regularly.

One day he turned up already drunk. He could hardly walk. I refused to serve him the bottle of whisky.

The following day, I was waiting for him all day. He didn't turn up so I decided to stroll down to his house and knocked the door. No answer. I informed the neighbour about it. Later in the evening I had a telephone call from his neighbour that the police broke the front door open and found him dead.

An elderly man living in a caravan in the woods not far from our business used to come to our post office every Saturday morning. He used to be rich, used to own coal mines. To some he used to be super rich, yet the hands of the devil were long enough to catch those who were destined to die. One morning he didn't turn up for his usual trip. And he was found dead in his caravan.

My list of such experiences could be enormous for the devils who lived with us, the devils we fought and the devils that those people lived with and eventually surrendered to in the end. Death is inevitable and life is a gift, which gives us the opportunity of hope to build our karmic account to settle the final bill and attain divine freedom.

When the social distancing ban is over, and we are walking with a sense of gratitude for being alive, hugging those close to us, you can choose whatever path you want, but for me I am ready to leave behind the painful past and strive to learn to live with peace and harmony. And I dedicate this book to humanity striving for the peace and harmony for our future.

PEACE AT LAST

I hear the gun shot.
Nothing unusual for the place.
I move on.

I see barbed wire extending far and far as far as my eyes
can see.
Nothing unusual for the place.
I move on.

I see morning sunshine manoeuvring its way through
beautiful peaks of mountains.
I see thick frost melting down from the tip of the twisted
barbed wire
to the thirsty ground.

I hear the gun shot.
Nothing unusual for the place.
I move on.

I see the barbed wire extending far and far as far as my
eyes can see.
Nothing unusual for the place.
I move on.

I see children playing
I see birds chirping.
I see animals grazing grass.
I see beautiful flowers.

I hear the gun shot.
Nothing unusual for the place.
I move on.

I see the barbed wire extending far and far as far as my
eyes can see.
Nothing unusual for the place.
I move on.

The giggling of the children.
The singing of the birds.
The smell of freshness of grass.
Still in my breath.
The fragrance of flowers still in the air.

I hear the gun shot.
Nothing unusual for the place.
I move on.

I see the barbed wire extending far and far as far as my
eyes can see.
Nothing unusual for the place.
I move on.

Soon the barbed wire ends.
Soon the gun shot ends.
Happy faces.

Men, women and children and the usual crowd.
Sweetness of freedom.
I move on.

The sun is still shining on me.
But soon the darkness creeps in .
The night sets in.

All things disappear.
Just some noise here and there.
And then... an emptiness....
An emptiness... until morning.
I see sunshine manoeuvring its way through beautiful
peaks of mountains.
I see thick frost melting down from the tip of the twisted

barbed wire

to the thirsty ground.

All things reappear.

I see a beautiful lake.

I throw a stone and watch...

ripples of water appearing and reappearing. On and on.

There is a continuity.

And in that continuity, there is discontinuity.

And in that discontinuity there is peace.

In between gun shots there is silence.

All wars end in peace.

The barbed wire ends in freedom.

Between two dark nights,

there is a beautiful day

Day of hope, happiness, peace and freedom.

The world out there is a mirror reflection of the
world within.

All life experiences are the phenomena of our mind
perceiving the diversity and multiplicity of objective
world.

Our minds create thoughts

like the ripples of water in the lake.

In between our thoughts there is discontinuity.

And in that discontinuity lies peace.

If you can hold on to it, that peace is...

THE PEACE AT LAST.

CLOSING REMARKS

I am blessed with four grandchildren; Aanya, Joshua, Dylan and Alex. They are all great. When Aanya was six years old, I wrote a little story on her birthday. The story goes something like this:

Once upon a time there was a king. Powerful and angry. The king had a daughter. He loved her very dearly. She had everything she needed, and she got everything she asked for. And why not? She was the princess. The king would call her, 'My beautiful princess' always. The princess, too, loved the king very dearly.

One day the princess was feeling very poorly. She was sweating. She was vomiting and had a severe headache. The king came rushing. On his way he shouted, 'Doctor! Doctor come and examine my beautiful princess. She is not well. She is not well,' he yelled out of desperation.

'Yes your majesty I have examined her and given her medicine. She will be fine soon,' the doctor assured him.

Soon the princess was fine. Happy and playing. The king was happy too. But it was not a happy ending. She was poorly again. She was shivering. She was sweating. She was vomiting and she had a severe headache. The king came rushing to her and shouted on his way, 'Doctor, doctor! Examine my beautiful princess. She is not well. She is not well,' he yelled again.

'Yes, your majesty I have examined her and given medicine.'

'But you said the same last time and she is poorly again. You must do something, you must,' the king told the doctor in a loud, angry voice.

'She has malaria declared the doctor.'

'Malaria?' roared the king.

'Yes, your majesty. It is caused by being bitten by mosquitoes.'

'Mosquitoes. Soldiers! Soldiers!' he ordered, 'Go and kill all the mosquitoes in my entire kingdom.'

The king's order must be obeyed. The soldiers with their guns and swords went and killed all the mosquitoes wherever they could find one. 'No more mosquitoes,' the soldiers declared.

Once again, the princess was happy and playing and the king was happy too. But then, this too, was short lived, as the princess became poorly again. She was shivering. She was sweating. She was vomiting and she had a severe headache. The whole palace was in deep sorrow. The king called a special meeting with all his personal advisers to find a solution. The problem they were facing was that the mosquitoes were everywhere; in the woods, in the trees, in the stagnant water, on the leaves and everywhere. They keep coming back as soon as they are destroyed.

Everyone in the palace was very unhappy, especially the king himself. Seeing the king so unhappy the princess was very sad too. She was sitting alone in her room, tired and exhausted. When she looked up, she saw a bright light touching her tears on her cheeks from above. She was very happy as she had seen the bright light before which was like a friend to her in times of need.

The bright light came closer to her ears and whispered a few words of wisdom and soon the bright light disappeared in the air. The king's beautiful princess never had malaria again. They all lived happy ever after.

The significance of the story is the power of 'bright light' from the angelic world.

$$E = m\,c^2$$

'E' = energy, 'm' is mass and 'c' is the speed of light.

Peter Russell a nuclear physicist says that the light at the end of a tunnel is so bright that it drives us all on. It's not just a fantasy. Its gaining momentum. It's the key thing.

Einstein's 'Theory of Relativity' explains the nature of light. The speed of light is 186,000 miles per second. This is constant. But time and space change. At the speed of light your mass becomes infinite. But light, still, travels with the speed of light so the light is beyond time, non-local and has no mass.

During a meditative state, apart from experiencing divine light, our sense of time, space and mass seems to dissolve. There appears to be some parallels between the speed of light in the physical world and that of our consciousness.

It appears that light is the first step towards manifestation of something. Whatever the fundamental nature of reality is, light seems to be the key thing.

Even if you haven't understood everything in this book, I suppose what I'm trying to say is, be encouraged to understand yourself and the world around you better. Don't be afraid to think differently. Think about yourself and the part you play in society, the world and even in the whole cosmos. Don't be scared to push the boundaries of thought. Look at the big picture and then the even bigger picture. Life is full of too many coincidences and karmic activity to be purely dictated by just formulas, equations, textbooks and societal norms. Not everything is black and white – so be curious about the grey areas in between and connect yourself to everything around you. You are part of everything, and you always will be.

EPILOGUE

It was a Sunday afternoon, a warm and sunny afternoon in Portsmouth where my daughter Radha and her husband did their undergraduate degrees. A family weekend out. A long walk along the pebbled beach led us to... guess where? An Indian restaurant. In recent years Indian restaurants have become very popular in the UK for its sophisticated taste and origin. We are a family of four grandchildren, one English son-in law, one Irish son-in-law and the 3rd Son-in-law of Indian origin and of course a Welsh son, Indian wife and myself a British citizen of Indian origin. The grandchildren consist of two Irish boys Alex and Dylan, whom I very proudly call Dylan Kumar Ryan as he carries my second name KUMAR. Then there is my granddaughter Aanya Rani Camps who carry my wife's middle name" RANI". To me this creates an ideal post-colonial family for any healthy family discussion with diseased post-colonial syndrome. We support and value each other despite our usual family arguments and I am quite happy to call it a "HAPPY FAMILY". Yes, we are finally here for our evening meals. As I glanced through the menu, I lead the menu and shouted if everyone agrees on Pani Puri for starter. Yes... yes... but I wanted to reconfirm with Chris. I knew he likes Indian food hot or very hot but Pani Puri. I didn't think else was shouting it's YUMMY. ITS YUMMY... ITS PANI PURI. They all agreed... yes it's yummy it's... PANI PURI. So it was Pani Puri for starter and it came soon enough for me to show a demonstration. I grabbed a round Pani Puri with my left hand, made a hole with thumb, dropped a few pieces of vegetables and filled with spicy water. Pushed it all through my mouth opened as wide as possible. Chris repeated the whole process like a postgraduate biochemistry lesson. The whole thing exploded in his mouth. The scene after was not very pleasant. There was spicy water all over his face his head his forehead even his ears How did you manage that? I asked Chris. His eyes were red, and he was coughing as if someone has saved him from drowning in the sea. Everyone was laughing and giggling. I was feeling so sorry for him, I am sure the others felt the same despite how they reacted. "Sorry Chris we shouldn't have let you go through this." To which he replied rather chuckled in his own voice. "All I could see was a huge mushroom like they showed in BBC programme last night explaining the dropping of atomic bomb on Nagasaki and Hiroshima."

This reminds me of another explosion, not because it has happened recently, or I heard about it through our parents and grandparents. But it's fundamental to humanity and took place at a time when science can throw some light on it. A time when the existing elementary particles gases, energy, fire, water took part in some kind of gigantic explosion... "THE BIG BANG".

WHO AM I?

The most common word I have used so far is the word "I" itself. Yet we do not know much about it. PERHAPS ITS ONE OF THE HARD PROBLEM OF SCIENCE TODAY. Does anybody really know? I can hear the melodious noise of the water following its way through rocks, I can see the sun shining on the surface of the river and the waves. I see the other side of the bank, its vague, but I know it is there. Like it has always been there ever before.

Wait! Wait! I just had an accident. I just collided with a tree... tall and solid. Yes, I can even see the bird sitting on one of its branches. Hang on a minute. Where is the bird? Where is the tree? I am not stupid. I just passed them. They must be there. Like it has been there. Like it has been there. Ever and ever before.

It's getting darker and darker and I must get back home. As I walk along the river, the air along is getting fresher and breezier. Everything around is getting hazier and I can hardly see the other bank of the river, as beautiful as this one. Like it has always been there ever and ever before.

I drive a car. The hand brake, the clutch, the gear, the biting point. And the car moves. Not only moves but reaches its destination without much of my involvement, taking the right exit at the round about turning sharp right by the chai shop. Who is actually driving the car? Is there someone tiny inside me? Like it has been there forever and ever before.

The path I am walking on, the road I drove on, the air I breathed will follow on to the next. The moon, the sun the sky and the mountain they will all reappear tomorrow like it has been there before.

I reached home. I can hardly see myself, forget my hands. But my fingers know very well, where the switches are! With a click a button, there is light everywhere. Everything was right back nice and clear, shining everywhere. I can, even see my pussy cat who has been hiding from me for my attention. Like she has always been there, ever and before.

She jumped on to me. As I brushed my hands over her furry body, she pushed herself in, within my arms, as if she has a long story to tell... that someone punctured one of my back tyres... that the dead leaves from the next door was all over our house and needs clearing, like year before and before.

And of course, there was some kind of tension around the house.... a family quarrel. I was tired and exhausted and wanted to go to bed early - in no mood for an argument. I want to go to bed early. I am hungry and am going for a wash. I sat down for my meal. As if I was sitting there forever and ever before.

I saw my little pussy cat staring at me. Maybe, she was asking for her share of milk. I called her with my little secret sign. She jumped onto me, sat by my side but refused to drink any milk. Then she moved away. The whole situation was getting unpleasant. This reminded me of an ancient Indian story, every time a visitor comes to a house, offered a meal with suspicion and someone has to sacrifice one of the senses in genuity of food.

That's what I normally do to avoid such situations. After a quick meditation and a cool breeze through the window. I felt relaxed and I slept. Soon I was in a pleasant state of dream... on a train journey in India, which I did make in early seventies perhaps. How can I forget that train journey? A man following me from behind, well built, tall, with white shirt and black trousers. It was a sleeper, and the journey was for over 12 hours. Yes I left behind a typical crowded train; with every one of us having our own unique story to tell filled with mixed feelings of sorrow, distress and pleasure; leaving behind an empty station for the next train with passengers of their own stories. Only thing permanent was, I.

OBSERVER, foreseeing every activity under all circumstances. Yes it was a sleeper train and a long 12-hour journey with overnight sleeping facilities with food and drinks. I must try to make extra effort to be friendly with people around. Had a quick look around. Not too bad, thought to myself. Mixed kind of people. I can deal with that. I remembered some well-rehearsed versatile well-cushioned words, like, chacha ji for middle to seventy, dadaji for over70, beta, beti for minor's mummy ji or bahan ji. I can manage that. I was dying for a cup of tea. Remember the golden rule. NEVER SWITCH THE LIGHTS ON WITHOUT PERMISSION. Very carefully I managed to take out my thermos flask out of my precious little leather suitcase. Even managed to whisper to offer to others. "You can switch the lights on if others have no objection." I was on a right path, I said to myself. Made sure that no one is interested in my tea, I quickly finished my tea with couple of rich tea biscuits which I always enjoy half dipped in the tea. The train was fast and was shaking with some kind rhythmic movement of the tea in the cup. I had enough practice in the past and I knew very well if I count up to 1.2.3. it can go straight into my mouth with maximum pleasure. I most certainly did not want it to fall down as the poor old man next birth down was a balled headed man. Very quickly, I re organized everything back into the suitcase as I was getting ready to retire to bed. All carefully locked safely. As I was about to sleep I suddenly remembered the chain with a lock at the end, which I bought at the previous station. I tied the handle of my precious little leather suitcase with the thick iron rod running between the two births. I was happy and satisfied with myself. After all it was my first ever journey of its nature which I must prove to myself and to others. As the lock   clicked in I was even happier. Now to find a safe place to keep the ring with key at the end, so that no one can find it accept me in the morning. For a moment I thought of throwing this out of window. Nobody will know where the key is in the morning except me. How clever!!! OH NO, OH NO. I AM NOT THAT STUPID. BUT THEN I FOUND A PLACE... A SECRET PLACE AS I WAS GOING INTO MY SLEEP STAGE... DEEP SLEEP STAGE. I AM NOT GOING TO TELL YOU. NOT TO ANY BODY EXCEPT TO MYSELF. YES!! TO MYSELF.

As a child I used to love watching the train passing by in a speed with a loud whistling noise. Though not allowed, we used to play around the railway line. One of the most exciting and courageous things to do was to place a coin on the railway line just before the train and let the train pass by. The coin was elongated. I used to show the same to my friends in school and enjoy their amusement. There was some kind of rhythm between the noise of the train, the noise of the whistle of the train, and my brain shifting back and fore from drowsiness to sleep to dream to deep sleep and back to drowsiness.

Soon enough it was morning. Morning enough for me to have wakefulness, though still drowsy. No one around to offer tea or coffee to bring me up to a good wakefulness. As I was trying to experiment the manifestation of guess what? I couldn't find the key to the chain, which was locked to the iron bar. I panicked. My panic level still went further high as my destination station, I realized, is only half an hour away and I can't find the key. So that was that something from my memory in the past. Where the hell I put the key rind?. How does it relate to my playing around the railway line while speedy trains pass by in my early childhood? Funny but not funny anymore.

As a student of science, I always found it very exciting to observe the son and the moon, the stars in the sky and the entire cosmos and its enormity. Millions and millions of galaxies and stars juggling around the universe in perfect harmony. The sun, the only source of energy radiating round absorbable only by chlorophyll cells in green plants... the primary consumer. The rest, entire animal and plant kingdom derived energy as a secondary consumer in a small organelle in each cells of our bodies called MITOCHONDRION by a special mechanism through which energy is transferred from ATP (adenosine triphosphate) to ADP a molecule of energy is released for various body activities. A cell is a fundamental unit of life. There are trillions of cells in a living organism, each intricately balanced to each other and to the rest of the cosmos. Each of these cells have several organelles responsible for various body activities, shelf sustainable. Each and every cell in my body knows what other cells are doing in or outside my body. Apart from these organelles each cell contains very sophisticated system of hereditary materials in the nucleus of each cell. Exciting as it was, my first journey to explore living cells with my teacher opened up my yet another dream. A dream of another living and colourful world with Amoeba to insects to mosquitoes to living world of butterflies. Once again a shelf evolving, shelf sustaining system.

Yet on the other hand there are a system of inorganic system, equally interesting and puzzling to scientists and philosophers of the time. No matter what we know of science today and no matter where we stand in term of our understanding of science, technology, philosophy, sociology and theology, I am quite happy in my science, in my mind, and explain various things as they appear to explain to me in the day-to-day logic. This opened up a new dimension of science. Everything and a anything is may is made up of small molecules called atoms. These small atoms are held together by a web of energy called electrons, protons and neutrons. The electrons are positively charged particles, protons are negatively charged, and neutrons are neutral in their electrochemical behaviours. We as a human race have evolved over the years so is the science technologies in conjunction with our frontal lobes of our brain. The humanity today, owes to science and technology. Sir Royal Albert Einstein is my hero and our society owes to scientists like Sir Isaac Newton and many like him today, for their contributions to science and technology. We can go back to our libraries and tear off all our text books, we can destroy all our research from the past and declare them invalid, dead and buried. But I can't deny their contributions. I can't deny that they too have burnt their fingers while counting starts at night.

As I was taught in my schooldays, I have no problems in accepting that the whole cosmos is made up of a composite of living and non-living substances attracted to each other by an electromagnetic force. And each of these molecules are made of even smaller particles called electrons, proton and neutron separated by large space. Yes large space, large enough space to explain an ever-expanding space and time. In a room like my bedroom, I have more space than matter as my tables, desks and furniture, which itself has lot of intermolecular space. In fact, they say one of the largest building in United States, if it brought down can mount to only a small grain of rice as matter. The modern-day Quantum Physics goes on further to explain that, even these electron, proton and neutrons have another dimension of life where the solidity of an object collapse. In my previous book vol. 1 I have tried to explain how an electron, solid, as may appear to lose its solidity when an independent observer try to measure it. Weird, but true from scientific point of view. Maybe so but it goes hand in hand to account for a surplus of energy as predicted by supporters of BIG BANG. The field of energy produced by the BIG BANG created an ever-expanding electromagnetic field if possibilities... field of infinite possibilities... THE CONSCIOUSNESS.

Modern day science THE QUANTUM PHYSICS as described by nuclear physicist Professor Amit Goswami and others goes even further to explain that everything the materialistic world we experience is nothing but energy. The solidity is an illusion created by our minds. If we consider the whole cosmos as a big, large lake with no physical boundaries and the objective world in it with its interpretational experiences are the individual units of consciousness, as represented by the waves of ripple of consciousness. Each and every activity of the brain and mind are the phenomena of the mind civility as it expresses itself as physical and emotional world. A group of men women is gathered together outside the village with guns in their hands in order to celebrate Dussehra which happens to be the same day as a baby is borne in the village. The guns went up in celebration but no FIRE... It's a girl and not a boy!!! NO... NO... NO... The whole universe trembled with a big noise of a high-speed train, which pierced the heart of the entire cosmos. Yes I heard the noise of the same speedy train with high whistling noise... NO... NO... NO... Leave me alone... I don't want to go. The whole universe trembled with a big noise of a whistling speedy train, which pierced the heart of entirety. I cried and cried but the steam engine with loud whistling noise had no feelings on its own. I hear a cold and cruel feminine voice, "Don't worry, he will be alright, let him cry for some time." My existence kept on sinking in me and soon enough I was like a drop of water falling from sky, strong but ready to fight. Ready to surrender... a complete surrender to the vastness of the ocean.

I was declared dead at the ROYAL GLAMORGAN HOSPITAL after three consecutive cardiac arrests. I can see myself inside the coffin, which is in a queue for cremation. The people gathering around the queue are the family and friends for their last respects. As the queue progressed, nearer to the gate, the father performed a candlelight prayer.

Our prayer was not successful, and my coffin was pushed away for the next day. It was a funny looking place. I was confused with no family and friends around. I could see nurses and other health care staff, but they could not communicate. I cried and cried for help. But no one could hear our voices. Later on, in the night I realized that, perhaps there were two different wards, one attached to ours while the others with the normal ward. The coffin proceeded as planned that morning and I landed up in a strange place with trees and people around walking with no purpose, here and there. I was sleeping on a tree on a branch. I could see them in small groups, singles and doubles roaming around without any purpose. Perhaps that's it for me. That's what destined for me. But to my greatest surprise I see my angel wife climbing up the tree. How did you do that? I yelled. She was hiding behind me in the coffin she said in her confident voice. "As I rubbed my stomach she read my mind, "I have seen places serving food. Let me get some for you."

I could not get much of a sleep last night. Grabbed a cup of coffee out of desperation to go to sleep. Wrong! One of my friends told me. Never drink coffee to go back to sleep. It has caffeine in it, if at all this keeps you awake. Next morning, I woke up with less wakefulness. I had three meetings and I needed more wakefulness. Had some extra caffeine and pushed off without making as little noise as possible for my wife who was fast asleep next to me. I was feeling tired and exhausted. I could not have made to the entire day. I rang my wife home and decided to have a day off. After lot of persuasion, we agreed to have lunch together and then go for cinema. Had a quick lunch and then we were in cinema by 12.30. It was one of her favourite film but, somehow I was not getting that kind of feedback. I put my left hand round her neck to show my affection. O.M.G. !!! I was holding someone else's hands round her neck. I got shock of my life. The cinema screen in front was blank. I just managed to stay in answering my own doubts for the past few weeks. Waiting for her early morning wakeup calls. Empty pendant case on dressing table. Extra few centimetres of smile with lunch... and so on. Did you know that man sitting next to you in the cinema hall? I asked her after morning coffee. Y E S... there was a coolness in her reply and then the coolness breaks into chilling I c e... He is Amit... A nice guy... You must meet him some time. And we both continued with our conversation as morning progressed. By the way, we didn't have to have day off and we both continued with our normal days' work. We both were sleeping in our bed side by side until morning.

WE ARE SPIRITUAL BEINGS HAVING A HUMAN EXPERIENCE

The traditional way of thinking is that there is a body. In that body there is brain. And mind is the extension of the brain. On the other hand, consciousness is the field of unlimited possibilities. Mind is the extension of the consciousness. An ignorant mind is a pure field of unlimited possibilities. It is nonlocal, is everywhere and has no space and time. It has not thought, no emotions, no excitations of any kind. As soon as a thought arises, mind is created in the field of unlimited possibilities. This mind, then, manifests my world of experiential reality. In the same way we all create our own realities, unique to each of us as manifested by our own thoughts. As someone said, "I AM BECAUSE I THINK I AM". Mind thinks. My mind creates about 50 to 70 thousand thoughts per minute. Lot of thoughts. There are millions and millions of galaxies and therefore may be millions of BIG BANGS to produce them in the past and in future. Each time a thought arises from the field of unlimited possibilities my existence is created. Before any one from the Deep end or science jumps in and starts arguing, let us try to understand the principle of "DO BE

DO BE DO." by Professor Amit Goshwami. Ayurveda has been used to treat any illness in the past by herbal materials derived from medicinal plants. When the younger brother of Rama, LAKSHMAN was injured, Monkey God Hanuman was sent to the jungle of HIMALAYAS to bring sanjeevan I buties. A plant material to treat Lakshman. He brought the whole section if the mountain containing the plant. The idea is that the plant alone is not so important, they say. It is the intelligence within. I can understand the importance of Big Bang in creating our universe or multiverse as they call it these days, what about the role of the intelligence which perhaps existed before the Big Bang, which perhaps entangle us all with the whole universe.

So, there is a body, in that body there is a brain, mind is the extension of the brain and then there is consciousness with unlimited possibilities. On the other way round there is consciousness a field of unlimited possibilities, mind is the by-product of the consciousness and then there is brain which interact with experiential bodily manifestation of the world of reality as we perceive. The consciousness seem to be common and is the source of all potential and potential only and nothing... NO...THING. The problem we may face is to accept that how can something arise from nothing, even though is only a stimulation of biochemical nature. On the other side of the coin is consciousness again with enormous possibilities. The biochemical excitation of the mind can be relatively easy to explain the interaction. A NASA Scientist Thomas Campbell, in his book "MY BIG TOE" describes individual units of consciousness or SOUL as our unit of consciousness. What I am trying to do here is to understand a relationship between the manifestation of my illusionary world as perceived through my mind through explosion of many varied forms, existing substances of the moment, the consciousness; the soul consciousness and the intelligence which entangle them together within and beyond the horizon of our space.

According to a BBC documentary program few months ago the understanding of soul consciousness as unit has been there for over a century. The story of ST Licuana boy James and his parents as described in the program cannot be ignored and the idea of soul and reincarnation cannot be left under the carpet even by modern day scientist. In Mahabharata once Lord Krishna opened His mouth wide and the whole world saw the entire universe in it. That the speed of light is constant. The Einstein Theory of Relativity opens up many questions about mass, energy, space and time. I think that there is still room for scientists, theologians, the historians to join together for a common pursuit.

The ancient Indian wisdom upanishad is one of the oldest teaching which goes far beyond and describe consciousness in its original sense. Swami Sarwapriyananda explains that, when I see a scene through my little eyes I become seer and the scene become seen. When I drive a car through my two little eyes I become the driver through my mind I drive the car. I see through my eyes, but my eyes are the seer. Seer and the seen are distinct from each other. My little eyes are not the driver. I am the driver through my mind. My mind sees the object not the eyes. The eyes do not see the object but is aware of what is happening out of all its experiences through all the senses. My mind through all my senses create all the realities of my own little world and then I see and perceive. Yet I am not the mind. I am distinct from seer and the seen. I am independent observer illuminating the world of my existence created by my mind. I am only the witness of the body and mind. I am consciousness on which I shine on to manifest my reality. I am not an object. I am consciousness a subjective world on which I shine to illuminate my world of reality. The world of my objects. Swami Sarwaprianandan goes on to explain further to say that I am not an object I am consciousness which shines on to create reality by a simple story. There are ten monks travelling towards village. On the way they had to cross a river. After crossing the river, they had a head count and found one missing. They were only nine. A passer-by stopped and saw them crying over this. He knew exactly what was happening. He volunteered to solve the problem. He raised his forefinger one by one on each and counted up to nine but when it came to 10 he curved the same finger back towards himself. And they all were very happy to find the 10th monk. The turning back the 10th finger is the KEY POINT here. I am the 10th, I am the independent witness which shines on all experiences and create my own world.

When I am awake; I am the Waker; When I am at Sleep; I am the Sleeper; When I am in dream; I am the dreamer; When I am in deep sleep; I am the deep sleeper. But I am always there experiencing all the experiences in all the stages. Call it a Soul, Call it Atman, Call it Brahman; Call it just a pure consciousness Or may be just ENERGY. Lord Krishna said, I am GOD, I cannot be extinguished by water. I cannot be blown away by wind. I cannot be cut by any weapon. I am always there... indestructible. Bashar has been channelling through by Darryl Anka for over 35 years. He puts forward 4 basic laws of creation.

1. That I exist. And once I exist I am always there.

2. All is One And One Is All. Meaning God created us, and he is also a part of the creation.

3. What I put out is what I get back. Physical reality is the mirror reflection of what is within me.

4. Only thing is constant in the universe is CHANGE. Meaning everything changes from one form to another. All energy is, however, a constant. There is nothing other than energy. ENERGY is the key player in the years to come.

Soul .. atman .. consciousness .. mind .. brain ... thought .. peace is the silence between thoughts and mind is the excitation of peace in my consciousness created by my thoughts. Mind is the subjective world whereas brain is a part of my own creation the objective world like any other part of the body. I am here, at an interesting junction and have a choice to make. The subject object split. The brain is of objective entity, consciousness, on the other hand is a pure subjective phenomenon. The question is canning the subjective world of pure consciousness create mind and then create its own thought and the objective world including the brain. Meaning something from nothing. Or can the brain cells interact with the pure consciousness to produce mind, which can then create thoughts and feelings and respond to it. Meaning something from something.

THE BANYAN TREE

How can I forget my local village where I grew up from my early childhood and from where mv y journey of life began. A small village with no school, no hospital, not even a temple, forget about a bar or cinema or a community place. Some mud houses and some brick houses and huts too. People of all ages, castes and tribes; some butchers, some labourers, some cobblers, some vegetable growers.

People living in the house behind was a small shop run by two brothers selling all the essentials from rice, lentils, oil, kerosene oil, spices, children sweets and many other things. I heard that the two brothers tried to stab each other, quite recently. The lady living in front of our house have been in alcohol making business for some time. They used to make sell alcoholic drink made out of boiled MAHUA (a wild fruit) or juice from palm tree early in the morning before sun rise.

We were not allowed to go to their houses or mix with them.

On one side of the village there was a big Banyan Tree and a pond, again in an elevated ground. To me, with hundreds and thousands of coloured threads hanging on the trunk and the branches this was our school, our temple, our playground, our community hall, our place to connect my soul to the Spirit world. In fact it is said that LORD BUDHA got his enlightenment under a Banyan Tree near Bodhgaya in India. In fact, this was our social, cultural and religious platform for many occasions. This Banyan tree is a witness to all matrimonial services, religious festivals, financial disputes.

Or legal disputes in time of good or bad. In time of draught or flood. In time of financial crisis or health endemic like coronavirus, we gathered here and prayed. They say, if you pray with your body mind and soul in harmony God listens.

There was a famous Indian story writer named Munsi Premchanda. I read this story a few years ago. The following story is based on that.

TREE AND A POND ON AN ELEVATED GROUND WAS ANOTHER IMPORTANT FEATURE OF THE VILLAGE.

It's a story about an old lady and her landlord. And of course, the five wise men of the village. The old lady was a weak and vulnerable member of the community while the landlord was young energetic businessman. He owned plenty of land wealth and power. He always walked with his two bodyguards with guns in their hands wherever he went. By his mere look, tall, well-built and long moustache, he looked very intimidating. No one dared talk against him. The complaint was that the landlord had occupied her land unlawfully whereas the landlord counter argued that the old lady had been growing crops and using products for years without paying any rent. It was time they did something about it, and all were waiting for something to happen.

People started gathering with nervousness. The chief, an old man sat in the centre respectfully. On the other hand, four of his advisors asked of the villagers to keep coming, they all were curiously counting the number of people joining each side. It was getting more and more obvious. One by one both sides were called on the platform for any documentary evidence. Then there was a chance for general public for their comments... A silence... A complete silence...

The chief, the old man who has to announce the final decision was sweating. The verdict was declared, "The documentary evidence were not convincing. Then, on compassionate ground I declare the decision in favour of the old lady. She can use the land as her own till a satisfactory documentary evidence are established. The guns were fired in anger in the sky. Once again, I could hear the noise of speedy train with loud whistle piercing the heart of entire cosmos. The chief the old man could not bear the burden of the trauma. He died of a heart attack. But he was hailed, he was praised, and his decision prevailed even long after his death.

REFERENCES

1, Gregg Braden (Born 28 June 1954). An American author and scientist who is widely known for linking science and spirituality. He became noted for his claim that the magnetic polarity of the earth was about to reverse Braden argued that the change in the earth's magnetic field might have effects on human DNA. He also argued that human emotions affect DNA and that the collective prayer may have healing physical effects.

2, Deepak Chopra (Born October 22, 1946). Chopra studied medicine in India before emigrating to USA in 1970. In 1985, he met Maharishi Mahesh Yogi and became involved in the Transcendental Meditation Movement. He, then became the Executive director of Sharp Healthcare's centre for Mind Body medicine. In 1996, he co-founded the Chopra centre for wellbeing.

Dr. Chopra believes that a person may attain a perfect health free from diseases. An idea, which has been heavily criticised by scientific communities. Seeing the human body as undergirded by a quantum mechanical body composed of energy and information.

Chopra speaks and writes regularly about metaphysics, including the study of consciousness and Vedanta. Consciousness is both a subject and an object. It is consciousness that creates reality. Socially induced conditioning separates us from rest of beings. Intention is the key. Our body is some total of all our intentions, thoughts feelings and emotions and so is our minds.

3, The story of sati savitri;

It's a story of the power of love of Savitri for her husband Satyawan in Satyuga found in Vena Parva (The book of the forest) of Mahabharata.

4, VEDANTA by Swami Sarwapriyenanda;

Vedanta is a philosophy taught by the veda, the most ancient scriptures of India. Its basic teaching is that our real nature is divine. God, the underlying reality, exists in every being. Religion is therefore, a search for self-knowledge, a search for the God within. It is a Sanskrit word meaning "end of knowledge". A compound of two words veda meaning knowledge and anta meaning the end... the conclusion... the highest teaching of vedanta. Self realisation is its essence. UPNISHADS are the source of spiritual knowledge while vedanta is the cutting edge.

5, Prof. Amit Goshwami (Born 4th November 1936 in India). Amit Goswami, PhD is a retired professor of theoretical physics at the university of Oregano. He is the pioneer of the new paradigm of science called science within consciousness. Consciousness is the ground of all beings. Consciousness is nonlocal. Consciousness collapses in materialism... a theory of duality... a theory of unlimited Quantum. How can consciousness being a field of unlimited possibilities collapses into actuality and yet being the phenomenon of the brain?

     Quantum physics says that every thing is a possibility. How possibilities transform into actualities? Interaction of particles during upward causation do not solve the problem of transformation of actuality into consciousness, the unlimited possibilities. How the brain being the phenomenon of dualism where energy is constant sends signals to the consciousness. Just does not work. While in downward causation where brain is the extension of consciousness, it does not need any signal.

Is there any way where informations can be transferred between brains? That's the question... signal less communication. Non local phenomenon of consciousness.

Theory of creativity. Do be do be do practice. Doing and being. Doing takes place in consciousness while being is a part of subconscious mind. Downward causation has elements of freewill so intention influences the manifestation of reality. Spiritual practice needs ego.

Self realisation is powerful and when that happens. You then surrender the Ego. Without ego there is no creativity. Self realisation... creativity... quantum leap.

Brain and consciousness. How does brain sees a flower? The consciousness collapses to observe the brain. The same consciousness collapses to experience the brain. Perception creates memory and memory creates perception. For the brain observer is the observed.

The hierarchal entanglement. The quantum leap and the theory of Darwinian evolution explains the material aspect of evolution by natural selection e.g. the car, TV, mobiles and so on. It does not take into account values unless you change the market. Market values like love and peace.

6, J. Krishnamurti. (1895-1986). The perfume of a flower is in the flower. The very flower itself is the essence of the perfume. Thinking is part of memory and our brain is the instrument.

Experience, knowledge, memory and the response of memory is thought. Experiencer and the experience are the same. Like the observer and the observed. Thinker is not separate from his thought. Thought is based on experience, knowledge and memory and the reaction of memory is thought. Consciousness is the accumulated experience, knowledge, beliefs and memory over the generations.

Consciousness is unlimited activities of thoughts, which is not personal but is of human kind. Time is an illusion created by the movement of thought. So when the observation is pure. Pandawas and kaurawas. Arjuna is filled with moral dilemma and despair about the violence and death the war will cause in the battle against his own kin. He wonders if he should renounce and seeks Krishna's Counsel, whose answers and discourse constitute the Bhagwat Gita. Krishna counsels Arjuna to fulfil his kshatriya (warrior) duty to uphold Dharma through 'selfless action'. The Krishna - Arjuna dialogues covers a broad range of spiritual topics, touching upon ethical dilemma and philosophical issues that go far beyond the war Arjuna faces.

8, Swami Vivekana da (12 January 1863 - 4 July 1902) born Narendra Nath Dutta was an Indian Hindu monk from Bengal. He was a key figure in the introduction of the Indian philosophies of Vedanta and Yoga to the western world. He was a major force in the revival of Hinduism in India and contributed to the concept of nationalism in colonial India. He is perhaps, best known for his speech in which he introduced Hinduism at the parliament of the world's religions in Chicago in 1893.

148

9, Dr. Bruce Harold Lipton (born 21 October 1944) is an American developmental biologist notable for his views on epigenetic. In his book 'The Biology of Belief' he claimed that beliefs control human biology rather than DNA and inheritance. In 1971 Lipn received his PhD in Developmental Biology from the university of Virginia. From 1973 to 1982 he taught anatomy at the University of Wisconsin School of Medicine, before joining St George's University School of medicine as a professor of anatomy for three years. Lipton, sometime in 1980s rejected atheism and came to believe that the way the cells function demonstrates the existence of God.

10, Peter Russell (born 7th May 1946) educated in University of Cambridge, went from being a strict atheist and scientist to discovering a profound personal synthesis of the mystical and the scientific. He blends physics, psychology and philosophy to reach a new world view in which consciousness is a fundamental equality of creation. Integrating a deep knowledge of science with his own experiences of meditation, Peter Russell arrives at a universe similar to that described by many mystics, one in which the inner and the outer worlds no longer conflict. The bridge between them, he shows, is light and he invites his readers through his books to cross the bridge to find a new meaning in God and deeper significance in spiritual practices.

11, Bashar, born 12 October 1951, Ottawa, Canada.

12, Thomas Campbell (born 9 December 1944). 'The My Big Toe' doesn't represent the pride of authorship but is a book in which Tom is referenced or has contributed a chapter, CONSCIOUSNESS

149

Bridging a gap between Science and the new super science of Quantum Mechanics.

ACKNOWLEDGEMENTS

There is a long list of people who contributed in the manifestation of this book. It's not possible to name them all. However, there are some I can't help but mention:

Neha, my daughter (Dr Neha Singh) who kept a detailed account of day to day ups and downs in my time at hospital of which I was completely unaware of, for almost a month. The chapter 'Roller Coaster Ride' is her ingenuity.

My son Rahul was always there in every step of the way during the entire journey in helping me with typing, dealing with my laptop and mobile, inspiring me with his thoughts and encouragement. The cover of the book is his design and it represents the theme of the book beautifully.

I cannot forget my daughter Radha and her husband Chris in helping me with printing the draft copy.

My eldest daughter Rashmi has always been supportive and helpful in various ways throughout, especially in introducing me to a suitable publisher... Mr Dave Lewis from 'Publish and Print'. I am deeply indebted to him for his excellent services in proof reading, formatting, editing and in bringing the book to such a standard for readers and for myself.

I cannot forget my wife Anju, as always, for being my Guinea pig in listening to my writing chapter by chapter in between making tasty curry and rice.

I am also grateful for my associations with Amita and Helena from Brahmakumaris, Cardiff for introducing meditation to me.

My appreciation also goes to Darpan for marketing the book and Darragh for his helpful comments and encouragement during the course of writing.

And finally...

During the war between Lord Rama and the evil King Ravana in order to liberate Sita, wife of Lord Rama, captured by the king Ravana, the king of Lanka. They decided to make a bridge of stones between the southern most coast of India and Sri Lanka (then called Lanka). The stones started to float as soon as RAMA was written on it. During the process of building the bridge, a group of little squirrels joined together, went to the sea, had a dip in order to wet their furry bodies, rolled over in the sand and then went onto the bridge, shook the sand off the body hard, to fill the gaps in between the stones to make it smoother for Lord Rama to walk on the bridge. They kept on doing this again and again. My grandchildren Aanya, Joshua Dylan and Alex were like those little squirrels making me feel good about writing the book, no matter how hard the journey was. Reading the draft copy and helping me create images and drawings. So sweet. I had to do it .

Published by
www.publishandprint.co.uk

Printed in Great Britain
by Amazon

63417716R00092